MW00453518

This Side of Broken

Purpose in Pain

Freedom in Forgiveness

God bless you Julia

By

Dana Gailey

Because of the cross...
Dana Gailey
7/19

To Chris, Parker, and Trent Mays who walked
with me to this side of broken.

This Side of Broken: Purpose in Pain - Freedom in Forgiveness

Religion / Christian Life / Spiritual Growth

ISBN-10: 1548870951
ISBN-13: 978-1548870959
Religion / Christian Life / Spiritual Growth

Contents

PART 1: PURPOSE IN PAIN

Chapter 1 Fiery Trials, Really?......................... 11

Chapter 2 To Know is to Believe................. 21

Chapter 3 Something is Broken.................. 27

Chapter 4 He Will Answer....................... 39

Chapter 5 God is The Healer.................... 47

Chapter 6 Let it Go!............................ 55

Chapter 7 His Provision...His Purpose......... 67

PART 2: FREEDOM IN FORGIVENESS

Chapter 8   Get Me to Morning.................. 77

Chapter 9   Reasons to Forgive 83

Chapter 10   If I Don't Forgive................... 91

Chapter 11   Bitterness............................ 99

Chapter 12   Three Forgivenesses................ 105

Chapter 13   Forgive for Love.................... 119

INTRODUCTION

Life brings joy and life brings sorrow. Yes, sorrow comes, and with those sorrows come our questions. In spite of the questions we may have, God is with us. Amy Carmichael, a beloved missionary to India explained, "Faith does not eliminate the questions. But faith knows where to take them."[1]

When I found, myself raising three boys alone, I had lots of questions for God. I thought I was the only Christian woman in America flying solo. Not so today, but I was the only single momma I knew. Through that time, I learned from my boys that my greatest opportunity to capture their hearts for Christ was my being willing to allow Christ to capture mine—right through the middle of our pain.

They have said to me, "Momma, I never saw you cry." I did cry, though. I must have held back a million tears. I cried into my pillow at night and in the shower in the early morning.

God saw every tear.

Every single tear.

In retrospect, I should have had a good cry with my boys more often. Perhaps it would have helped them sort through some of their own sorrow. But I knew the importance of peace. Though it was not always possible, I tried to shield them from the gale winds the best I could. God's sweet grace got us through. God's loving grace will get you to this side of broken, as well.

I had to let God in close . . . just God and me. The evidence of His work in me was gentle change, even if it was three steps forward and two steps back. No change was more important than me learning to believe in God's love through pain and the journey

---

[1] *A Chance to Die;* Amy Carmichael

to forgiveness. I learned then that pain and forgiveness are inseparable. I'm still learning that.

As I wrote these pages God showed me new things about forgiving others. He told me to look back, all the way back, and to forgive. When I wrote about asking for forgiveness He told me to write letters to a few folks and send them that very day. So, I did. Finally, in writing about trusting Him through the fire, looking for His love in pain, He intermittently provides refining fires for us.

Oh, those refining fires . . . those scary, heartbreaking times.

Why fire, Lord?

As I look back I realize that it wasn't during times of peace and plenty that I learned to trust God, but through the fire. I learned to whisper prayers all day long and as I fell asleep at night. The words I read in my Bible became my Bread of Life. It was then that the Lord began to show me how much He loved me and how hopeless I was apart from Him.

My confidence had to be in God. There was no other way. I had no checking account because the bank fee just about covered milk money for the month. No shopping—except for school uniforms or groceries. I figured if we didn't see it - we wouldn't want it. Our simple life made our faith simple. We had no backup plan. I determined that God was seeking after our best, and if He loved us with an all sustaining love like the Bible said, I could trust Him.

Through the toughest of times and the greatest of sorrows, I can hold onto and have confidence in God's love. The word is *hesed* in Hebrew. It means loving kindness, a loyal love.

I like that.

My Father in Heaven *will* work all things for good because I am called according to His purpose as He is making me look like Him (Romans 8:28, 29). My Father *will* turn my ashes into beauty (Isaiah 61). He *will* complete the work He has begun in me

(Philippians 1:6). He *will* use me to display His splendor (Isaiah 61) to draw a hurting world to Him - which is God's purpose for having me here.

God is faithful. He loves me. In times of blessing and in pain I can rest securely in His loyal love for me, and so can you. The Psalmist reminds us that God knows our sorrow. "You've kept track of my every toss and turn through the sleepless nights. Each tear entered in your ledger, each ache written in your book" (Psalm 56:8 The Message).

He has counted every tear.

He knows.

No doubt you have some broken places in your heart. We all do. As you read through these pages, move at your own pace. Take your time; let God into places in your heart to which you have never given Him access. Allow Him to pour His sweet love into your broken places. As you do, you will know perhaps for the first time how much you are loved and understand the power in forgiveness. There you will find peace and freedom.

Part 1
Purpose in Pain

1

Fiery Trials—Really?

"Fiery trials make golden Christians."
(Charles H. Spurgeon—19th century English preacher)

I picked up the frame sitting on the desk and read one of the quotes and scriptures in our home. This one, written by Matthew Henry was a favorite. "If I am not on the plain of conflict, I am a well-equipped coward." I dropped the frame in the drawer and closed it.

I thought, *Lord, I'm going to put this baby in the drawer, because I don't think I want to be on the front line anymore. I am tired, body and soul. Surely, we have met our plain-of-conflict quota for the past decade. We are trying to walk with You and we are getting slapped around thoroughly. We and our children have walked through war, death, disease, deception, divorce, slander, and financial disaster. Calf-rope, Father, calf-rope.*

When I was a little girl I would watch my big brothers wrestle on the floor or in the yard. When one of them had enough he would yell "calf-rope!" A calf with its legs tied can do nothing but give up and lie there. That's where I was. I'd had enough. Charles Haddon Spurgeon would not have been very proud of me that day. I wasn't doing so well at being a golden Christian.

God?

In my pain?

Really?

Yes, God was. He's always teaching me something if I am listening. My heart was deflated from the battering. I felt weary and hopeless. But His love was at work. It's scary, but my pain is a part of the tapestry of my life. It is part of God's perfectly planned universe. Yet it makes no sense to us unless we look at it in the shadow of the cross - the bloody cross of Jesus.

Pain and forgiveness.

They are inseparable.

Unless we feel pain through offense, we have no idea what this forgiveness thing is. We have no need to take up our cross, to die to ourselves, and follow Jesus. Unless we have felt pain through offense, we won't grow more like Him so our lives will shine for a hurting world.

Our world is fallen and it groans from the effects of sin, and without purpose it is hopeless. But God's intent for our lives and those watching us is sure. It's certain, and pain is a part of it. The way we navigate pain and failure teaches our children and a watching world far more about the love of God than how we whistle through sweet times. God won't leave us where we are. He will move us along one way or another. He loves us that much.

Yet, it is hard to understand this when we see the horrible effects of natural disaster. There is no way to make sense of parents burying their children or the horror of physical, emotional, or sexual abuse. How can we weigh the cost of families torn apart and hearts ripped open? Who would have thought the 21st century would produce child sex slavery on almost every continent, genocides of entire populations, murder through abortion of over sixty million babies in the United States alone, and more Christians being killed for their faith than in any other time in history? The creation does indeed groan with the effects of sin (Romans 8:22).

Psalm 23 describes sorrowful times as the valley of the shadow of death. Not physical death, but so despairing that it is a valley like death. Attacks on the innocent, abandonment, divorce, abuse, devastating illness, or the death of loved ones kills a piece of our hearts. Our Lord Jesus also experienced utter despair as he anticipated the hours before Him and the sacrifice for the sins of the world. He cried out, "(My) soul is overwhelmed to the point of death" (Matthew 26:38).

This was Jesus' valley of the shadow of death. He walked this dark path before us.

Just like Jesus, in the absolute depth of despair our pain will not be wasted.

God promises He will "comfort those who mourn, and provide for those who grieve in Zion—to bestow on them a crown of beauty instead of ashes, the oil of gladness instead of mourning, and a garment of praise instead of a spirit of despair. They will be called oaks of righteousness, a planting of the Lord for the display of his splendor" (Isaiah 61:2b-3).

God loves us and will exchange beauty for our ashes, and because we have been touched by hurt we are more able to touch a hurting world. "Praise be to the God and Father of our Lord Jesus Christ, the Father of compassion and the God of all comfort, who comforts us in all our troubles, so that we can comfort those in any trouble with the comfort we ourselves receive from God, for just as we share abundantly in the sufferings of Christ, so also our comfort abounds through Christ (2 Corinthians 1:3-5).

Just like Jesus.

That's how we display His splendor with a message of hope (Isaiah 61) and love at work. He is completing the work He has begun in us (Philippians 1:6). This good thing growing in us, this righteousness, takes time. An acorn that falls to the ground will over time grow into a mighty oak tree. Growing into oaks of righteousness - God completing the work He has begun in us - takes time. God's sweet time.

Proverbs 4:18 reads "Righteousness is like the first gleam of dawn shining ever brighter until the full light of day." The first time I read that description of righteousness I smiled inside and read it again.

And again.

It describes an out-of-this-universe thing happening in every child of God who allows Him access to their hearts.

First Gleam of Dawn

Darkness
The alarm
Down the stairs
Coffee's on
Cup and verses in hand, I head outside
Tucking my legs under me taking a sip of coffee

I wait
And wait

Slowly, silently
Amazing
A glimpse of light
From night to day
The edge of magnificence
Rays bursting forth to eternity
Through pastels and fluff
Bright, clean, clear

Pure light
Blinding brilliance
The full light of day

Every morning God gives us a living color picture of what He is doing inside us. Through good times and bad, through His love, righteousness is growing in us. Through time and yes, through some pain, we're growing up so we will impact our world for Christ.

It seems when I am trying to do what God wants me to, I am often slammed the hardest from the enemy of God. When I am moving forward, perhaps to a place I have never been before, I can feel it. It may come from a person or circumstance totally out of my control, no matter how hard I try to reel it in. When that happened recently, Romans 8:28 popped into my mind. "All things work together for good to those who love Him and are called to His purpose."

All things, Lord? Are you really going to use this awful thing for good?

I believe You are.

That promise has given me the courage to get up and go on when I wanted to crawl into a corner and curl up in the fetal position. Romans 8:28 tells us what He is doing, and Romans 8:29 tells us why He is doing it—He is changing us into the likeness of His Son. "For those God foreknew He also predestined to be conformed into the likeness of his Son." It sounds like a fairytale, but it's not. It is there for the taking.

In *The Message,* 2 Corinthians 3 reads, "Nothing between us and God, our faces shining with the brightness of His face. And so, we are transfigured much like the Messiah, our lives becoming brighter and more beautiful as God enters our lives and we become like Him."

In our deepest sorrow, we decide if we believe this.

God called us by name and paid for us with the life of His Son. He's making us like His Son so others will come to know Him. He won't waste one sorrow. He's about eternal business. Though at times we feel like insignificant specks in eternity tossed about by circumstances, God is with us. He knows us. He loves us.

God knows we're broken. He's the only one who can put us back together—if we allow Him access to our hearts.

Yes, if we *allow* Him into our hearts. Many times, I have missed the message God has for me through pain. But I want to listen for His voice and never miss that message again. Although it is hard to listen when we are hurting, God is speaking to us. We can ask Him anything. He can handle it.

Finding Purpose in This Mess

1. What questions do you have for God? This life in Christ is about relationship. Talk to your Father. Tell Him what is in your heart. Ask Him any questions you have. God hears your cry.

2. Are you tired in your soul? Are you going through a time when you want to give up and yell "calf-rope!" because circumstances are hard and unfair? If you are not going through it now, do you remember a time when you found yourself in this place? What is or was going on?

3. How do you think God can use your pain to draw you closer to Him? How is it possible in the pain you've experienced that you could learn what forgiveness really is?

4. What is God's promise in Romans 8:28?

5. What is His purpose in Romans 8:29?

Paul wrote this promise to the first century church in Rome. They were dying for their faith in Jesus Christ, and he wrote them to give them perspective and hope. When we can't make sense of our pain this promise gives us perspective and hope.

You may have learned this promise when you were seven years old. You may not know it at all. Knowing it is one thing. Believing it to be true is quite another. Read Romans 8:28, 29 over and over and ask God to make these words real to you...to the very depths of your heart real to you. I am not saying the relentless ache in your heart will go away today. But I am asking you to begin to *believe* what God's promise is to you. This is where the rubber meets the road. This is where we stand out as different from the rest of the world in our response to life.

When we *choose to believe.*

6. A majestic oak takes a century to grow. Am I willing to wait on God's time? Will I let God work in me and those around me as He forms me into an oak of righteousness? How am I fighting God's love working in me and those around me?

7. Read Isaiah 61:1-3. Though the promise of restoration in Isaiah 61 is to the Jews who were destroyed in judgment for their sin, it is for us, as well. That's why Jesus came.

In verse 1, what is God's promise to the broken hearted?

What is God's promise to the captives?

8. We know why our hearts are broken. But do we know what might be holding us captive? What might we need freedom from?

9. In verse 3, what does God want to do with our pain? Can you believe that?

Lord, help us take You at Your word.

2

To Know Him is to Believe Him

How can I believe God can work all things for good? How can He restore my loss? How can I believe He will complete the work He has begun in me? We trust those who speak truth. We trust those with proven character. We come to trust them by getting to know them well. In knowing our Lord up close and personal - sweetly and deeply- we will believe Him.

We were created for relationship, first with our Father in Heaven, then with people - a parent, a spouse, a sister, a brother, or a friend. When we get to know someone well, we can talk with them about anything. We can share our joys, our dreams, and our heartbreaks. It is also true that the more we spend time with someone, the more we are like them and share similar ideas, values, and attitudes. We even use their words.

I had the distinct privilege of homeschooling one of my granddaughters for a few years. We were inseparable most days as we worked through Bible, English, History, Math, and Science. I have noticed something. Brooke's good taste and eye for beauty rubbed off on me. She is perhaps one of the most creative people I know, and she has made me more creative. What has she acquired from me? Grammy-isms exactly as I say them. I chuckle to myself when I hear my words coming out of her mouth.

Yes, when we spend time with someone, we become more like them. Just as our children and grandchildren mimic our words, we want to mimic God's words. We want to know God so well that we can believe Him. The more we are with Him the more we are going to look like Him, and the primary way to get to know Him is through His Word.

Our faith in Who He is and the depth of His love for us grows through His Word and by His Spirit. Love, joy, peace, and purpose grow as we learn His Word. Each bit of the Word of God in us is a bit more of God in us. For this reason, the devil will fight to keep us from learning the Bible. Jesus prayed for the disciples, "Sanctify them by the truth, your word is truth" (John 17:17). Jesus knew that through His Word they would grow into His image. They would be free then to do the work to which He had called them.

There are many ways to get the Word of God into our hearts. Though it is certainly not my favorite method, just as for the disciples, many of God's words were forged in my heart through the fire. But praise Jesus there are other less painful ways, as well. Some of us can easily learn scripture by reading or saying the verses. For some though, memorizing can be difficult. One night I stumbled onto a way to learn scripture which has helped me greatly. It might help you, as well.

When I was staying with my grandchildren that evening I saw note cards and pieces of paper with letters written in vertical lines. I thought perhaps someone was going a little nuts around there. But my son, Chris, explained to me that it was Kristi, my daughter-in-love's, method for learning the Bible.

I tried it. It worked! This is how I do it. I write the scripture at the top of my prayer journal page. Then I write the first letter of each word in vertical columns going down the page. I read the scripture through numerous times. Each day or as often as I can, I run my finger down the vertical columns while saying the scripture a few times. It's not long until I have it.

Whether you use vertical letters or not I encourage you to let God renew your heart and mind by filling it with His words. Throughout these pages, you will see many scriptures with vertical letters below them. I pray that they might open your heart in new ways to God's word.

"It is written: 'Man shall not live on bread alone, but on every word that comes from the mouth of God'" (Matthew 4:4).

And

"Then Jesus declared, 'I am the bread of life'" (John 6:35).

Yes, Jesus is the bread of life. However, you choose to, get to know your Father in Heaven sweetly and deeply by learning His words.

Hide His words in your heart!

1. "And we know that in all things God works for the good of those who love Him, who have been called according to His purpose. For those God foreknew He predestined to be conformed to the image of His Son," Romans 8:28, 29.

A	G	W	A	F	T
W	W	L	T	H	I
K	F	H,	H	P	O
T	T	W	P.	T	H
I	G	H	F	B	S.
A	O	B	T	C	
T	T	C	G	I	

2. "Being confident in this, that He who began a good work in you will carry it out on to completion until the day of Christ Jesus" (Philippians 1:6).

B	T	A	Y	O	U	C
C	H	G	W	O	T	J.
I	W	W	C	T	D	
T	B	I	I	C	O	

3. "He has sent me to bind up the brokenhearted, to proclaim freedom for the captives, and release from darkness for the prisoners . . . to provide for those who grieve in Zion - to bestow on them a crown of beauty instead of ashes, the oil of joy instead of mourning, and a garment of praise instead of a spirit of despair" (Isaiah 61:1b-3a)

H	T	D	G	O	I	O
H	P	F	I	B	O	A
S	F	T	Z -	I	M,	S
M	F	P.	T	O	A	O
T	T	T	B	A,	A	D.
B	C,	P	O	T	G	
U	A	F	T	O	O	
T	R	T	A	O	P	
B,	F	W	C	J	I	

3

Something Is Broken

*A broken heart is just that—broken. It hurts as the grief of death . . .
but God.*

As I write these words, hunting and pecking my way along, I
need God's healing touch. Because of a recent accident, God has
brought me to the place that I can write with more passion,
tenderness, and some degree of understanding.

Our son and his family took my husband, Don, and me out for
a lovely dinner. On the way, back to the car I stepped back, fell,
and broke my arm. More specifically I crunched the bones in my
wrist. It could have had something to do with me wearing some
adorable black shoes with cute little heels!

I realized almost immediately that my tender throat and
oncoming head cold were just part of my challenges in the weeks
to come. Though we didn't know about this detour, God was not
taken by surprise. He never is.

I share this example of pain knowing fully that the depth of
some of your pain is beyond imaginings. I can only exemplify with
this analogy because I have experienced and can compare it to my
valley of the shadow of death. If you are hurting right now, I must
first say I am deeply sorry for your pain.

I continue to learn that pain changes us. Pain throws us at
God's mercy. It shows us things we have needed to see about God
and about other people. Often our pain reveals hidden places in us
that are broken.

It Hurts

I sat in the emergency room with my pitiful-looking arm propped up on my coat whispering to my husband, Don, "Don't touch it. Don't touch it. Don't touch it." Something was broken . . . Something I could not fix. How often we are in desperate need of help yet refuse to let God or anyone else in close enough to help us.

Don had driven us toward town as I emphatically stated that I needed to go home and get some ice. He replied even more emphatically, "What we need to do is go to the hospital. We can't fix this." I wanted to go home and ice my arm. Yet if I had let it mend with bones out of place, it would have never been right.

That happens with hearts, too.

Often, we won't let God or others in close enough to help us when our hearts are broken. We pull away from help even though our hurt affects our witness for Christ as well as our relationships. Sadly, the relationships hurt most by our brokenness are with those we love deeply. We try to be okay, but we're not.

Blame Games and If-Onlys

Don and our oldest son, Chris, tried to figure out what in the world happened and mulled over the events leading to the fateful fall. However, I concluded that if I had only turned around instead of stepping back in the dark in those cute black shoes, I would not have fallen.

Nothing more. Nothing less.

Looking back, I realize there were times I wasted my pain looking for something or someone to blame. We can do all we know to live obedient, safe, and prudent lives. Yet we cannot prevent some calamity.

The blame game began in the Garden of Eden. Adam blamed Eve. Eve blamed the devil.

No, these are not the best role models to follow. Yet all too often we forget that we are God's precious possessions and we follow in Adam and Eve's footsteps. Instead of looking for someone to blame for our pain, we need instead to look to God for help.

Have you ever lost sleep by rehashing the if-onlys? I certainly have. When we descend into the if-onlys we look for someone to blame, even if it is ourselves. I eventually learned that the if-onlys are cruel and futile mental exercises. Jesus did not wring his hands with if-only or place guilt on His friends who fell asleep when he desperately needed their prayer. He didn't even blame His enemies. Our sin nature blames others, but as we grow in Christ we should be slow to point our fingers in blame. Blaming others is a sure sign that something is wrong in our hearts. Perhaps something is broken.

Time Stops
Time does a lot of things:
Time tells the truth.
Grows a man.
Or a tree.
Burns out a star.
And forms a canyon.

We are bound by its constraints minute by minute. But God isn't. I find great comfort in that. Sometimes, as in times of pain, God shuts everything down so we will, "be still and know (He is) God" (Psalm 46:10).

I had my plans for that week of November. That night after dinner I was going home to complete a monthly letter to the Military Prayer Chain for our church. That week I planned to crack and bag pecans, gather items for the troops, and send emails concerning a new women's ministry starting the next month. I also planned to sew more aprons for Caroline, my daughter-in-love, and do some writing if time permitted. After that, I was going to put some thought into Christmas preparations.

We make our plans, but everything can change in a moment. An accident, a diagnosis, a crime, a death, a natural disaster, or heartbreak, and plans come to a screeching halt. "In his heart man plans his course, but the Lord determines his steps" (Proverbs 16:9).

I learned that one purpose of pain is that it stops everything in our too-busy world. It stops the madness, leaving only God and us. Everything stopped that evening, and Don and I began the process of addressing the pain in my arm.

Bread and Water

"O people of Zion, who live in Jerusalem, you will weep no more. How gracious He will be when you cry for help! As soon as He hears, He will answer. Although the Lord gives you the bread of adversity and the water of affliction, your teachers will be hidden no more; with your own eyes, you will see them. Whether you turn to the right or to the left your ears will hear a voice behind you, saying, this is the way, walk in it" (Isaiah 30:19-21).

The people of Zion, the Hebrews, deserved the mess they were in. They turned their backs on God and lived the way they wanted. Isaiah encouraged them though. He referred to the hardships they experienced as "bread of adversity and water of affliction." He compared adversity to food and water which sustains life. He gave them God's perspective that these hardships were teachers guiding them toward Him.

The Lord now had my undivided attention. My pain was the teacher, and I was the student. Just like Isaiah's promise to the Hebrews, God heard my cry the moment I called. He drew me close to listen for His voice and to guide our steps. Even though my plan had abruptly stopped and God's plan ensued, the morning after the fall, I thanked Him. I thought about the thousands of times He had protected us. I thought of the mishaps that had *not* occurred because of God's gracious hand.

Dana to God:

"Praise You. And forgive me, Father, for taking your guarding hand for granted. Show me pride and self through this so You can sweep it out of me and make more room for You. And if You don't mind, Lord, I really don't want to have to learn this lesson again".

I ponder God's divine protecting wing ever covering us even as I sit here pecking out the rest of these pages with one hand. I am filled with gratitude that in the Lord's gracious and sovereign will my more capable left hand was free for the work set before me. *"Lord, don't let me waste this pain."*

Don't waste the pain in which you find yourself. Don't push away the healing power of the Great Physician even though it hurts greatly to move toward healing. His arms are open wide. If you run away from pain you will miss His amazing grace extended toward you. He really is nourishing you through it.

He loves you.

He is speaking to you.

Can you hear Him?

Finding Purpose in This Mess

Some of the pain deep inside is hunger pain, and I am not talking about a shortage of chips and salsa. There are many who are undernourished in the body of Christ. We are starving to death spiritually, wondering why we look for peace but can't seem to hold onto it for very long. Peace is in the pages of your Bible. Peace is waiting for you in those quiet moments you spend with God. There is no short cut. All other methods are counterfeits. We are talking about a relationship of love here, and relationship takes time.

1. We have learned a few things about pain and God's healing. Healing hurts, but if we don't let God in close we will never be whole. Is there something stopping me from letting God in close? Is there something stopping me from letting those who love me in close enough to help me when I am hurting? What is it?

2. We have lifelong thought patterns to which we default. Some of us can't enjoy life because we think, *if only I (or others) had done things differently, things wouldn't be as they are.* It is also easy at times to look for someone to blame. Satan tempts us to look at the glass half empty and to shake our fist at God and people when things go wrong. If we accept these lies, we consider ourselves victims. Do I struggle with any of these?

3. Cast these thoughts out with thoughts of what God says in His word simply with, "Thank You, Lord".

Write Philippians 4:6

Write 1Thessalonians 5:16,17

Write Colossians 1:12

4. What do these scriptures have in common?

5. Think of the faithfulness of God and of how thankful we are for His protection. An attitude of thanksgiving is God's idea. "Be anxious for nothing, but by prayer and petition WITH THANKSGIVING make your requests to God" (Philippians 4:6) and "Be joyful always, pray continually, give THANKS

in all circumstances, for this is God's will for you in Christ Jesus" (1 Thessalonians 5:16, 17). God doesn't tell us to be thankful because He's God. He tells us to be thankful because it works. It's not for Him. It's for us!

It changes our hearts. Gratitude begins the process of setting us free from our tangled thoughts. So, get a spiral notebook or journal and start a list of things you are thankful for like your children's smiles, warm water for a bath, or the sound of birds singing in the morning. Then when the if-onlys and blame games torment your mind, turn them into thank yous. Start your thank you list today. It will change you. It will change your family. The devil will hate it!

At times I have missed the best things of my relationship with God in the busyness of doing *His* work. But nothing stills me more quickly than a hefty dose of pain. Pain stops me in my tracks. In these times, I can hear God telling me things I have perhaps not heard before. God doesn't want to waste our pain, and He has great purpose in it if we will listen. Through the psalmist God reminds us to, "Be still and know that I am God" (Psalm 46:10). In times of hurt, are there things you have learned from Him that you could not see before?

6. We must open a book to read it. We must listen to our instructor to learn from him. To learn, grow, and even thrive in God's love through pain, we listen for His voice. Pain can nourish us. Look at Isaiah 30:20. What does Isaiah refer to as our teacher(s)?

7. Pray that the loving Father will open the eyes of our hearts to His healing touch so we can learn of His love through hurtful times. When we begin to experience His touch through pain, we can guide others to that healing touch, as well. How is this described in 2 Corinthians 1:3 -7?

8. Read Isaiah 30:15 & 18-21 a few times. What do you think God's message is? Write down the things He is telling you through these verses.

"Although the Lord gives you the bread of adversity and the water of affliction, your teachers will be hidden no more; with your own eyes, you will see them. Whether you turn to the right or to the left, your ears will hear a voice behind you saying, 'This is the way, walk in it.'" (Isaiah 30:20).

A A   H   S   T   B

T T   N   T.   T   Y

L W   M;   W   L,   S.

G O   W   Y   Y   T

Y A,   Y   T   E   I

T Y   O   T   W   T

B T   E   T   H   W

O W   Y   R   A   W

A B   W   O   V   I

                            I.

Do not be anxious about anything, but in every situation, by prayer and petition, with thanksgiving, present your request to God. And the peace of God which transcends all understanding will guard your hearts and your minds in Christ Jesus" (Philippians 4:6-7).

D	S,	R	T	M
N	B	T	A	I
B	P	G.	U	C
A	A	A	W	J.
A	P,	T	G	
A,	W	P	Y	
B	T,	O	H	
I	P	G	A	
E	Y	W	Y	

4

He Will Answer

I asked three things of those praying for me prior to surgery: First, I asked that I get a good stick nurse, one who would not chase my veins all over my arm before sticking in the needle. Next, I asked for wisdom for the doctors. Finally, I prayed for God's provision for an old girl who had not looked diligently enough for health coverage. While waiting to go in for surgery, I was thrilled and thankful when the nurse got the vein in the first stick. *Thank you, Lord.*

I lay there talking to the anesthesiologist about my head cold. He seemed a little concerned and checked for congestion in my chest. He began looking for a good vein under my arm to deaden it with a block. That made me nervous, so I told him in my croaky voice, "Just put me under and do what needs to be done."

As the sedative dripped into my IV I talked to God.

Dana to God:

"I can't do a thing about this, can I, Lord? I'm at Your mercy! Oh gosh, some of my drawers are messy. I hope I wake up from this surgery, Lord. If not, Don and the kids will have to dig through my messy drawers."

(Yes, I talked to the Lord about my messy drawers.)

God to Dana:

"You *can't* do a thing about this. I've got it though".

Zzzzzzz . . . Just when I think I'm tough and self-sufficient I am reminded . . .

I am weak.

He is strong.

I am at His mercy.

My second prayer request was met when the surgeon did a great job. An unusual looking plate and pins were inserted in my arm. My grandchildren later looked at the different views of the x-rays and agreed the plate looked like a cross between a big grasshopper and a dinosaur.

As the anesthesiologist left, I shut my eyes and whispered a prayer for me, my Don, our children, and theirs, and for the body of Christ. And, it didn't have anything to do with messy drawers.

It was Ephesians 3:16-19. "I pray that out of his glorious riches that He may strengthen you with power through His Spirit in your inner being so that Christ may dwell in your hearts by faith. And, I pray that being rooted and established in love that you have power together with all the saints to grasp how wide and long and high and deep is the love of Christ, that love that surpasses wisdom that you may be filled to the full of the measure of God." Fill them with You, Jesus, and fill me with You.

Two hours later I woke up.

I did wake up!

Don and the kids won't be digging through my drawers.

Though I was not speaking it out loud because my throat hurt considerably, I was again praying Ephesians 3:16-19. While totally helpless, my pain made me thirsty for God, and I had access to the throne of Grace through His word. Pain was the gift which brought

42

me to that helpless and wonderful place, and I got an up front and personal example of why we *hide* God's word in our hearts.

Allow Him to Heal Us, Heal our Children

Though the Great Physician desires to heal our souls, we often hide our deep pain - that is until God shakes it loose. His touch is the only way to wholeness, yet often we won't let Him begin or will not allow Him to complete the surgery of our hearts. We jump off God's operating table before His work is done because we fear losing control or being hurt more deeply.

We may be perpetually discontent. We can fall into depression. We might withdraw. Or we might stay mad all the time. Often to kill the pain in our souls we will change locations, friends, churches, spouses, jobs, or families. Until the break is healed though, no matter our environment, the hurt will follow us. The sources of our hurt will change names but the disappointment remains.

These recurring disappointments in us and others are red flags of warning. A red flag indicates something is wrong and needs attention. Our red flags are our Father in Heaven saying, "Let me love you, child. Let me heal your heart."

We prevent our Lord from doing His work in our children, as well, even grown children. Though God uses hardship to mold and grow us up, watching our children fail or hurt by others breaks our hearts. Often, we can't seem to allow our kids to make decisions, reap what they sow, or even fail - while praying them through the process.

We don't want them to hurt, and we care deeply about what others think of them. We might even be more concerned about our family's reputation than their holiness. Overprotecting and rescuing them can stand in God's path toward their holiness and

His nourishing them. Our rescue may deny them access to the Great Physician's operating room. We want them to be equipped to walk through trials under the wings of their loving Lord though, and no one can do a better job at equipping them than God.

Trust Them to Him

Christian parents often mirror the parenting of this age: afraid to trust God, we hold grown children too tightly, rescue them from difficulty, and manage them instead of releasing them to the Lord. How easy for these young people to then justify fleeing their faith in outward rebellion or hold a simmering, hopeless sorrow in their hearts hindering their ability to hear the voice of God for themselves.

There were nights I cried myself to sleep, because I so wanted to jump in and rescue my kids from hardships they were experiencing. Some hardships were of their own making. Some had been inflicted upon them. At times, I helped too much. Other times I helped too little.

Frenzied rescue is never God's will, though. Prayerful obedience is. When my sons were teenagers, I learned to talk less and pray more. When I remembered to zip my lip, they were freer to yield to the voice of the Holy Spirit for themselves.

Talk less.

Pray more.

God teaches them much more than we ever could.

Finding Purpose in This Mess

1. Is something broken? A red flag warns of forest fires. Two red flags warn of dangerously high waves in the ocean. A red flag on railways means stop, as does a red light. A red flag is a warning of impending danger, something not to be ignored. If we are honest with ourselves, are there some red flags waving around in our lives?

2. Recurring pain, frustration, depression, a need to control, and anger in our souls are all red flags. Could our pain be God warning us of danger? What is my first reaction to disappointment, a change of plans, or sinful people in my life? What do my reactions show me about myself and the things deep in my heart that only God can heal?

3. Am I a rescuer? Do I tend to rescue my kids or others too much? How? Or do I not help them through their struggles *enough?* What does that look like?

4. Read Ephesians 3:16-19 and pray for yourself and your family that each of you know how wide and long and high and deep the love of God is for you and that you be filled with His love. His love heals our broken places.

5. Use vertical lines to hide these words in your heart!

"I pray that out of his glorious riches that he may strengthen you with power through his Spirit in your inner being, so that Christ may dwell in your hearts through faith. And I pray that you being rooted and established in love may have power together with all the saints to know how wide and long and high and deep is the love of Christ, and to know this love that surpasses knowledge— that you may be filled to the measure with the fullness of God" (Ephesians 3:16-19)

I	H	A	A	O	T
P	S	I	T	C,	M,
T	I	P	S	A	W
O	Y	T	T	T	T
O	I	Y	K	K	F
H	B,	B	H	T	O
G	S	R	W	L	G.
R	T	A	A	T	
T	C	E	L	S	
H	M	I	A	K -	
M	D	L	H	T	
S	I	M	A	Y	
Y	Y	H	D	M	
W	H	P	I	B	
P	T	T	T	F	
T	F.	W	L	T	

5

God is The Healer

Healing Hurts

We don't want to hurt. We don't want our children to hurt. It's scary to think healing and growth have side effects which are usually painful. After my surgery one of my granddaughters asked me, "Grammy, did you cry?" "Yes," I said, "I did cry a few times." No, I was not enduring the horrific torment of cancer surgery and treatment or an organ transplant as friends of ours have. Nor had I lost a loved one to sudden tragedy as other friends of ours have. But I hurt. I couldn't keep anything down and couldn't handle the pain meds. So, I hurt. My sweet husband did all he knew but was helpless to fix it.

That left God and me.

Dana to God:

"Lord, I am sorry for being such a wimp."

There it is again.

I am weak.

He is strong.

He understands when I'm a wimp.

Healing Can be Ugly

I slept the entire first week after my arm was broken. But when the pain pills finally gave me consistent relief, I experienced vivid and horrifying nightmares. I decided this was God's way of not letting me get too comfortable with a narcotic. So, no more pain medication for me. I couldn't fix my hair and couldn't fit my swollen and wrapped arm into any of my clothes. So, I wore Don's XL tee shirts and looked like something the cat dragged in. Finally, my beloved neighbor, Marie, came to the rescue and gave me a cute haircut. That made me feel better at a superficial level, and I was on to the next step in the healing process.

Healing is a Process

For a while parts of my hand had no feeling, so it didn't hurt at all. When the nerves began to function again though, I had more pain. So, it is with healing deep in our souls. Some things we have experienced are so hurtful we have neatly tucked them away. Bringing these memories to the surface hurts far too much. Yet if we allow Him, God can heal even the deep hurt of our souls.

It was such a relief when the swelling began to go down. But there was give in the splint which allowed my arm to move. Again, it hurt. Don tenderly rewrapped it ever so tightly giving me relief from the pain. As our broken hearts heal and we hurt through the process, we too can run to our Father's arms.

He will hold us tight.

Just God and us.

Healing is Hard Work

The day the surgeon took off the splint, he said it was healing beautifully. Praise the Lord for no hard cast. The doctor began showing me exercises. My eyes bugged out as I leaned toward him. I was doing very well to hold my arm gently against my chest as my bones and joints seemed to be screaming. Sensing my hesitation, he warned that if I didn't have complete motion in a few weeks, he would send me to a physical therapist. A physical therapist hurts you and then charges you money for it. I was suddenly motivated to do my part, the hard work required to get this arm healed.

Allowing God to heal the hurts of our hearts is going to be a painful process and at times it will be ugly. We let Him in, and then we do our part, the work toward healing. His part is to do the surgery; our part is to daily walk obediently, doing whatever He tells us to do as we move toward healing. We re-address calamities to learn from them and grow in wisdom. We repent when repenting is needed. That is also a part of dealing with what's broken.

Though it may take some time, one day, we will wake up and be free.

Finding Purpose in This Mess

1. Dealing with the hurts of our hearts can be an ugly process. But God can heal us. He is able. There is no better illustration of this than the Samaritan woman whom Jesus spoke with at the well. Open your Bible and read of this account in John 4:1-42.

2. Jesus first talked to her about her need for living water, her need for Him. Then He got personal. What did He tell her in verse 16?

3. What was her reply in verse 17?

4. In verse 18 Jesus got to the real problem in her life. What did He say?

5. This woman obviously had great hurt in her heart causing her to go from relationship to relationship. We don't know how she had been hurt or what led to her choices, but Jesus did. We see that she didn't really want to talk about her 'stuff,' so she changed the subject and talked about where the Jews and Samaritans worshiped. But, Jesus brought the conversation

right back to her need for a Savior. What did the woman say in verse 25?

6. What did Jesus' reply in verse 26?

7. How did she respond to Jesus in verse 28, 29?

8. What was the result of her faith in verses 39-42?

The woman at the well learned that:

- Jesus is the living water.

"Jesus answered, "Everyone who drinks this water will be thirsty again, but whoever drinks the water I give them will never thirst. Indeed the water I give them will become in them a spring of water welling up to eternal life" (John 4:13,14).

- Jesus is The Messiah.

"The woman said, 'I know that Messiah (called Christ) is coming. When He comes He will explain everything to us.' 'I am the one speaking to you. I am He" (John 4:25, 26).

"Then, leaving her water jar, the woman went back to the town and said to the people, Come, see a man who told me everything I ever did. Could this be the Messiah?" (John 4:28-30).

- Jesus sets the captives free.

"Many of the Samaritans from that town believed in Him because of the woman's testimony. 'He told me everything I ever did'" (John 4:39).

Hurt people hurt people. Healed people help people. This woman's pain, her sorrow, and her subsequent life choices had probably hurt many folks. Then Jesus showed up. Jesus came to that well to reach into her hurt and heal her. He addressed her issues talking to her about what was going on in her life. Then He told her the Messiah she was looking for was right there with her at the well. The Messiah had come to set her free. In the same way, He has come to set us free.

Hide these words in your heart.

9. "Praise be to the God and Father of our Lord Jesus Christ, the Father of compassion and the God of all comfort, who comforts us in all our troubles, so that we can comfort those in any trouble with the comfort we ourselves receive from God, for just as we share abundantly in the sufferings of Christ, so also our comfort abounds through Christ. (2 Corinthians 1:3-5).

P	C,	W	C	F	O
B	T	C	T	G,	C,
T	F	U	I	F	S
T	O	I	A	J	A
G	C	A	T	A	O
A	A	O	W	W	C
F	T	T,	T	S	A
O	G	S	C	A	T
O	O	T	W	I	C.
L	A	W	O	T	
J	C,	C	R	S	

6

Let it Go!

To be free to share the love of Christ with her world, the woman at the well had to let go of the wounds of her past and see Christ for who He was. When she did, her eyes were opened to the truth. Our wounds are either for destruction, as is Satan's intent, or for the good of God's kingdom to touch a hurting world for Christ. The entire epoch of God and man, my life and your life, and the lives of our children are about God reconciling Himself to man through Christ's death and resurrection.

We make our faith complicated.

It's not complicated.

It's between me and God.

It's between you and God.

It comes down simply to each of us and our relationship with our Father in Heaven. It is only through Him that we will possess peace with God and the power that comes with it. What might be keeping me from having this possession, this peace and power Christ left for me? Could it be those things that I think I am entitled to?

What are my rights anyway?

Bear with me as I make a point. What about my right to a safe childhood? What about my right to have attention, affection, privacy, the big house, or my way? What about my right to have children, or not to have them, to have plenty of money to do the things I want to do, or to be understood? What about my right to a good paying job or my right to have a good father or mother, safe and healthy children, whatever I want to eat, or to do with my spare time? What about my right to stay young and be healthy or have a good retirement? Do you get my drift?

This has nothing to do with God's desire to bless His children, because He does desire to bless us. God is our Faithful Father. We are His delight and the apple of His eye. He loves to give us good gifts, and "Every good and perfect gift comes from God above" (James 1:17). Rather, it has to do with the condition of our hearts regarding what we think we deserve or don't deserve.

We may think, *"I sure don't deserve that and it will never happen to me"*. Having walked through the sorrow of a broken marriage, I was determined we would never see it happen again in our family—until it happened.

What do I deserve from God?

In the realm of justice before a holy God I deserve to go to hell. But Christ paid my way to righteousness. He did what I could not. He died for my sin. So then, what else am I entitled to?

Today, when we focus on the things we believe we are entitled to but have not gotten, we are choosing to be the walking wounded. Look at the way we live and place our priorities, our time, energy, passions, thoughts, or money. Think of what makes us anxious, angry, discontent, *or* filled with joy.

Give all these things to God.

All of them.

Lay them at His feet.

When we release expectations, rights, and perceived entitlements, the anger, anxiety, and discontent lose their place of importance. They do. In granting the Great Physician full access to our hearts we can be content with what we have and thankful for the Father's blessings.

The <u>gap between what we think we deserve and what we have will bear either scars inflicted by a destroyer or scars carefully placed by the Master Surgeon.</u> God's children experience pain just as our Jesus did. Saints of God like Elisabeth Elliot and Amy Carmichael experienced great pain accompanied by great faith.

Elisabeth Elliot

I can't talk about pain and forgiveness without sharing from the life of Elisabeth Elliot. Years ago, Elisabeth spoke at a women's event at our church. I couldn't wait to hear her words after reading some of her books and hearing her testimony. I was riveted by her trusting life of obedience. Her story forged deep faith in me.

The church was filled with women, so I sat in the back on the floor with Bible, pencil, and paper in hand. Listening and writing furiously, tears rolled down my cheeks as I remembered Elisabeth's story of submission, pain, and trust. One of her famous quotes is, "Where the will of God meets the will of man, someone has to die." I knew she had lived this many times. As was her custom at the end of each talk, the moment applause began; she quickly stepped off the stage and pointed her graceful finger up to her Lord.

I didn't know that day that one afternoon I would have the privilege of meeting her. I surely didn't know that I would cook meals for her and her husband, Lars, when they came to visit our friend, Margaret. I never imagined that one hot summer day

59

Elisabeth would sit prim and proper on our couch across from Don and me in our little house in Argyle, TX. A proper Bostonian, she might have been a bit shocked when I opened the door for her in my bare feet and wearing shorts. Yet my bare feet, shorts, and Texas drawl didn't seem to bother her at all.

The most endearing of the things I gleaned from Elisabeth's writing, speaking, and in meeting her was that she lived for an audience of One. She was not easily impressed with or surprised by much, because she was totally impressed with her God.

Elisabeth grew up an obedient daughter to her parents. In patient trust, she had waited years for God's perfect timing for her marriage to Jim Elliot. A short time later, Jim died a martyr when he was speared to death at the hands of those he was seeking to reach for Christ. Afterward, Elisabeth with her only child, Valerie, along with the other missionary women, moved into the South American jungle to love for Christ those who had killed her husband. Through the fearless obedience of these women, many in that culture were changed from cannibals to lovers of Christ.

Elisabeth's integrity and faith grew deeper through her pain and the scars it left. The Bible tells us, "Now we see Him in a mirror dimly, and then we will see Him face to face" (1 Corinthians 13:12).

We are going to look right into our beautiful Savior's loving eyes one day. But I believe we will recognize the greatest evidence of His love when we get our first glimpse of His scars. Breathtaking will be the scars of our Savior.

We are all scarred. We just have different scars. The bleeding will stop. The pain will subside, but scars will remain. They are supposed to. If we are willing, the Great Physician will make them our greatest strengths just like our Jesus' death on the cross. God leaves the scars and uses them to qualify us to help others with the same struggle.

Remember these verses. "Praise be to God and Father of our Lord Jesus Christ, the Father of compassion and the God of all comfort, who comforts us in our troubles, so that we can comfort those in any trouble with the comfort we ourselves have received from God. For just as the sufferings of Christ flow over into our lives, so also through Christ our comfort overflows. If we are distressed, it is for your comfort and salvation, if we are comforted, it is for your comfort, which produces in you patient endurance of the same sufferings we suffer. And, our hope for you is firm, because we know that just as you share in our sufferings, so also you share in our comfort . . . this happened that we might not rely on ourselves but on God, who raises the dead" (2 Corinthians 1:3-11).

Through pain, like no other time in your life, will you be able to identify with the suffering of Jesus. Like no time in your life will you be able to love others with the empathy of Jesus. You will never be the same and the scars will remain. What is amazing is that eventually scars are stronger than the skin around them. The harm or hurt we have gone through, or even a season of seemingly hopeless sin, once dealt with, repented of, and mortified, opens the door for the Lord to begin His work.

What if because of sin, Peter who denied our Lord, and Paul, who persecuted the saints, had not gone on? Yet, a repentant heart thrust them into the work of their lives. God will use these very struggles in sorrows or sin to help others again and again. It is pain that transforms us into those who "in humility think of others as better than ourselves" (Philippians 2:3). That is when the love of God pours out to the hurting world around us.

Elisabeth Elliot stepped over to the other side in the summer of 2015, but she had lived a life submitted to God. She outlived two husbands and in her last years after numerous mini-strokes she was unable to communicate at all.

God's love and words were planted deep within her though. While riding with her husband and Margaret one afternoon Elisabeth fell asleep. During her sleep, she began praying. Lars and Margaret had the privilege of listening as she spoke to her Lord beautifully in her perfect and proper way, not one misspoken word. The spirit of the living God was in Elisabeth Elliot's heart and nothing could take Him away. Nothing can separate us from the love of God.

Amy Carmichael

Another saint whose life impacted me greatly is Amy Carmichael. Amy spent a lifetime saving children in India, many from temple prostitution. In her early sixties, still tirelessly working for the Lord, she fell and broke her leg. This changed Amy's life dramatically. From that time until her death, almost twenty years later, she was in pain and confined to her home. Yet from her bed she counseled, loved, and continued to write influencing lives for Christ into the twenty-first century. *Hast Thou No Scar?* is one of Amy's poems, and it expresses her estimation of the Christian life.

Hast thou no scar?
No hidden scar on foot, or side, or hand?
I hear thee sung as mighty in the land,
I hear them hail thy bright ascendant star,
Hast thou no scar?

Hast thou no wound?
Yet I was wounded by the archers, spent,
Leaned Me against a tree to die; and rent
By ravening beasts that compassed me, I swooned:
Hast thou no wound?

No wound? No scar?
Yet, as the Master shall the servant be,
And pierced are the feet that follow Me;
But thine are whole: can he have followed far
Who has no wound nor scar?

Neither Elisabeth nor Amy wasted their pain. They allowed God to use their pain to bring them closer to the cause of Christ. This kind of trust in God is the only path that leads from where we are to where God wants to take us. That path is right through the middle of what we are walking through.

I have a scar on the inside of my arm about two inches long. It isn't very attractive but is a daily reminder of God's work in me. It was placed there by a surgeon who painstakingly fixed my broken arm just as God is lovingly and painstakingly healing the broken places in my heart.

Elisabeth and Amy, along with people like Joni Erickson Tada, who was paralyzed in an accident at seventeen, yet has ministered to millions, Nick Vujicic, born without limbs yet has touched lives for Christ all over the world, and Wess Stafford, abused by Christian workers as a child, yet served as president of Compassion International for decades, all had wounds. They had wounds like Joseph, Daniel, and Ruth of the Bible. Their wounds did not destroy them, however. Their wounds cast them into the arms of God.

If you have not read about the lives of these saints, I encourage you to get online, buy a book, or open your Bible and learn their stories.

They all had wounds.

They all had scars.

When the unthinkable occurred that wounded them and left scars, instead of cursing God, they chose to embrace Him. They were ordinary people like you and me who chose to believe God.

The century in which we live is both exciting and terrifying. It seems at every turn wrong is called right and right is called wrong. Worldwide, persecution of Christians is rampant and is creeping into every institution at every level in our nation. If our children walk in authentic relationship with Jesus Christ it will cost them much more than it has cost us. For that reason, may we seek to trust God like Nick Vujicic and Elisabeth Elliot and pray that our children will, as well.

Amid pain, we can trust the Master's loving hand guiding our lives.

We can.

Though it is hard, we are being transformed into tender and compassionate people who love the lost more than ourselves. "Heal me, O Lord, and I will be healed. Save me and I will be saved, for You are the One I praise" (Jeremiah 17:14).

Finding Purpose in This Mess

1. Have I (or will I) let the Master do surgery on the hurts of my heart? Have I repented of holding onto hurt as though it is an idol?

2. What do I need to do to let the Great Physician do surgery on my heart before I can then do the hard work toward healing?

3. Prayerfully consider all things to which you believe you are entitled. Our hearts will talk us out of most of these because the heart is exceedingly deceitful. Answer this question though, in a quiet and honest moment—just you and God.

4. Write out Romans 6:23.

5. What gift has God given us to replace our wages (what we deserve)?

6. Ask yourself, "Where are my priorities? Really, where are my priorities? Where is the greatest amount of time, thought, money, passion, and energy going?"

7. Do my priorities line up with God's? Are there some things that perhaps I need to let go and lay at the feet of Jesus? What might they be?

The choice is mine to let go of my expectations and demands on God and people, and rest in the joy that God saved me with great purpose. Jesus showed up at the well of my heart to heal me—if I will let Him. What do I deserve before a holy God?

"For the wages of sin is death, but the gift of God is eternal life in Christ Jesus our Lord" (Romans 6:23).

Yet, what does He give?

"Every good and perfect gift comes from God above" (James 1:17).

Though God's ways are not clear to me, one day I will see Him clearly!"Now we see Him in a mirror dimly, and then we will see Him face to face" (1 Corinthians 13:12).

7

His Provision . . . His Purpose

From the experience of my broken arm I learned one final lesson. Lest I be like the lepers whom Jesus healed yet did not return to give thanks, let me explain. God answered my third prayer request—for provision. I had been working on my cholesterol numbers which for several years had rendered me uninsurable. More than once, Don asked me if I had reapplied for insurance. Each time my answer was, "Not yet." I did not relish the idea of going through the application process only to be declined again. This was before government mandated healthcare or its alternative and I reasoned our budget was not ready for another insurance premium anyway. Therefore, I procrastinated, an action verb (or is that an *inaction* verb?) with which I am well-acquainted.

Beginning the Saturday evening after Thanksgiving, from that mis-step-moment to surgery two and a half days later, that inaction verb came home to roost to the tune of a $33,000 medical bill. Upon hearing the hospital alone would cost over $20,000, tears rolled down my cheeks and splashed onto my shirt. I was in shock and sad that I had been so careless and put Don and me in this situation. It may as well have been thirty-three million dollars. With the economy in decline and our building business a bust there was no way we were going to come up with this money.

Soon, though, I realized this was God's deal. I wasn't going to worry about this predicament and I couldn't wait to see what He was up to. About a week later He extended our faith when our beloved friend and neighbor, Margaret, walked across the street with a card of encouragement and almost a thousand dollars in small and large bills—a gift from the body of Christ.

Usually Don handles anything having to do with numbers, but I volunteered to step out of my comfort zone and communicate with those handling our healthcare balances. I began to make phone calls. I assured the billing agents that they would get the money they were owed, but only as we could pay them. I was sure it would take a long time.

During a call to the hospital billing office, I explained that we would send another payment next month. As we discussed totals, almost in midsentence, the agent paused and said, "Well, Mrs. Gailey, it looks to me like your balance is zero."

"Excuse me. What did you say?"

She repeated, "Your account balance is zero."

Then she gave me the account number. First, I presumed it must have been a small charge for my pink plastic pitcher. Then I reasoned it was a huge mistake. I told her I would talk with my husband and get back with her. Don was also in disbelief that any of these balances could possibly be zeroed out, yet the account number she gave me matched that of the gigantic hospital bill.

All I could do was cry. At the beginning of that phone call we owed these folks $23,000, but when I hung up we had no balance at all, and we never received another bill from the hospital or the surgeon. Yup, someone who makes those decisions zeroed out those balances. But, How? I have no idea, except we serve a great God. "With man it is impossible, but with God all things are possible" (Matthew 18:26).

I am not telling you that God will provide a money miracle in every case. God is not a genie. He is God. We have paid for automobiles, homes, doctor's bills, encyclopedias, a crazy expensive vacuum cleaner, braces, life insurance, health insurance, and a zillion other things. God has provided for us through prayer, hard work, the blessings of others, and yes, through insurance.

However, this time, apart from our efforts, God did it. On this day, He reminded me once again that every infinitesimal provision in life is a gift from Him. Every tiny thing we have He has provided, and in less than three weeks He provided $33,000 to pay the medical bills incurred because of my fall in the dark. God had me firmly in His grip even as I fell and broke my arm. He would use every moment of the experience to make me more like Him and to glorify His name. He spoke to my heart that if He wanted me to have something He would give it to me. Otherwise, He would not. He is my perfect Father who knows what is best for me. "God *will* meet all your needs according to the riches of His glory in Christ Jesus" (Philippians 4:19).

The last thing I learned from pain was that hopeless and desperate situations give us opportunities to see the miraculous grace of the God pour over us. He is the God of the impossible. It is undeniable. "With man it is impossible, but with God all things are possible" (Matthew 18:26). Only God can take our pain and ashes and transform them into beauty.

Unless a Seed Falls to the Ground

God's unchanging principles repeat themselves through His creation in people, plants, and animals—the entire universe. It is undeniably true that, "Unless a seed falls to the earth and dies, it remains alone but if it dies it bears much fruit" (John 12:24).

Life from death.

Just like Jesus.

My beautiful mother had a green thumb, and I learned a lot from her about growing plants. One of the most important things Mom taught me was that 'strategically' whacking my plants back makes them more beautiful. When I pinch off wilted blooms, fresh ones replace them. I cut lantanas and roses to about a foot tall in February when they are dormant. They look dead, but when the spring rains and sunshine come they burst into beauty. I pinch back the fronds of ferns and lovely fresh ones gingerly unroll and reach for the light.

From where does the beautiful growth come? It comes from below the cut. The cut is what forces the growth. And so, it is with pain. God strategically whacks us back. His intent for our pain is not to destroy us but to make us more beautiful for Him and to move us to that best place to impact souls for eternity.

Life from death.

Just like Jesus.

Purpose in pain.

"I am the vine, and my Father is the gardener. He cuts off every branch in me that bears no fruit, while every branch that does bear fruit He prunes so that it will be even more fruitful" (John 15:1,2).

Finding Purpose in This Mess

Throughout this study, we have looked at parts of 2 Corinthians 1:3-11. In Chapter 4 we put verses 3-5 in vertical letters to better hide these beautiful words in our heart. "Praise be to God and Father of our Lord Jesus Christ, the Father of compassion and the God of all comfort, who comforts us in our troubles, so that we can comfort those in any trouble with the comfort we ourselves have received from God. For just as the sufferings of Christ flow over into our lives, so also through Christ our comfort overflows.

Let's seek to hide the rest of this powerful truth in our hearts in verses 6-11. God won't waste one thing. My pain has made me a more patient person, a person who can endure the things this world throws at me. I am sharing in the suffering of my Lord Jesus and learning that I cannot rely on myself but only on Him. So I hide His truths in my heart.

1. "If we are distressed, it is for your comfort and salvation, if we are comforted, it is for your comfort, which produces in you patient endurance of the same sufferings we suffer. And, our hope for you is firm, because we know that just as you share in our sufferings, so also you share in our comfort . . . this happened that we might not rely on ourselves but on God, who raises the dead" (2 Corinthians 1:6-9).

I	A	Y	T	Y	Y	I	R	D.
W	S,	C,	S	I	S	O	O	
A	I	W	S	F,	I	C...	O	
D,	W	P	W	B	O	T	B	
I	A	I	S.	W	S,	H	O	
I	C,	Y	A	K	S	T	G,	
F	I	P	O	T	A	W	W	
Y	I	E	H	J	Y	M	R	
C	F	O	F	A	S	N	T	

2. Use vertical letters if you need them for the scriptures below. "Heal me, O Lord, and I will be healed. Save me and I will be saved, for You are the One I praise" (Jeremiah 17:14).

3. "I am the vine, and my Father is the gardener. He cuts off every branch in me that bears no fruit, while every branch that does bear fruit He prunes so that it will be even more fruitful (John 15:1,2).

4. "God *will* meet all your needs according to the riches of His glory in Christ Jesus" (Philippians 4:19).

5. "With man it is impossible, but with God all things are possible" (Matthew 18:26).

6. "Unless a seed falls to the earth and dies, it remains alone but if it dies it bears much fruit" (John 12:24).

Part 2
Freedom in Forgiveness

8

Get Me to Morning

My thoughts return to a night decades ago as my first marriage ended.

"So, this is a broken heart," I said out loud. "How can it hurt so much and I still be alive?" As I lay there I thought of a word I had heard for years describing my Lord, a word that until now I had not understood at heart level: "forsaken."

I asked, "Lord, is this forsaken?"

It was three in the morning and I had been lying awake through another night. Scripture I had memorized and used successfully to win past battles of the mind seemed far away. My marriage was over, and I could scarcely find God's precious Word inside me at all.

My thoughts raced. I felt numb. My senses seemed to be magnified. Even the light of the moon coming through the window made the ceiling texture look like a never ending inverted snow-topped mountain range pointing down and condemning me.

Tears poured onto my pillow. Yet through stinging eyes and silent sobs I felt Jesus' love for me more than I ever had. It dawned on me that He had not been forsaken by just one or a few but by the whole world. I thought, *"You were forsaken by the world, Lord. You were betrayed with a kiss. Your beloved friend, Peter, denied You before the third watch of the night like You said he would. Your disciples, the ones you hand- picked to walk with You, ran away. They ran away".*

Like me, people Jesus loved ran away from Him. His heart ached; His mind would not rest. He cried out, 'My God, my God, why have you forsaken me? Why are you so far from me, so far from the words of my groaning?' (Psalm 22:1). Jesus knew where I was. He had walked the path I was now walking. He knew how my heart hurt. So, I felt hope that He would get me and my precious boys through this.

Like Jesus, the moment before I felt His encouragement, I had felt far from God. I was a failure. I could see no value in my life. I wondered why I was even here - with no hope for tomorrow. Wouldn't the world be a better place without me?

As those thoughts passed through my mind, I *knew* they were lies. I immediately thought of my beautiful boys and listened for God's voice. Though I was walking through the valley of the shadow of death, He would get me to morning. I remembered David's words as he reminded himself of God's faithfulness. "Weeping may remain for a night, but joy comes in the morning" (Psalm 30:5).

God did get me to morning.

Every night He got us to morning.

When my flesh pulled my thoughts toward bitterness, I *fought* with all my heart to replace them with God's Words. I was determined I would not go that way. Not because I was all that spiritual. I was afraid of the alternative. I was afraid of the hurt it would inflict on everyone my life touched if I got stuck in bitterness. Both God's love and knowing that we would reap the seeds I sowed forced me through that hurt and anger toward forgiveness.

I had been raising my boys alone for a long time. Now it was official. Divorced was our new normal. With God's gracious help

80

I had to move forward. I knew I would find freedom only by striving to forgive. I understood forsaken at heart level, and I would begin to understand forgiveness at heart level, as well. As tough as it was to learn, what part could I have in the cross of Christ if I refused to forgive?

There is perhaps no greater gift we can grant those watching our lives than the gift of forgiveness. Pain is inevitable. We all experience it at times. But forgiveness is a choice. Matthew Henry explained it this way, "This [forgiveness] is not a plea of merit, but a plea of grace...Those that come to God for the forgiveness of their sins against him must make a conscious [choice] of forgiving those who have offended."[2]

Jesus simply told us to forgive so we would be forgiven (Luke 6:37).

---

[2] *Matthew Henry Commentary;* Note on Matt. 6:12

Finding Freedom

1. Have you ever had your heart broken? What was happening in your life then?

2. Have you felt like God didn't care about what you were going through? Why?

3. Jesus was disappointed by people. He was forsaken. Have you been forsaken or disappointed by people? You can talk to God about it. He will listen. What has happened?

4. David, the son of Jesse, was a faithful shepherd to his father and was faithful and courageous when Goliath threatened Saul's army. He was also faithful when King Saul summoned him to serve him in his court. Yet jealousy drove Saul to seek David's life, and though David had done nothing Saul chased him for years. Though at times David felt hopeless, he honored God by forgiving Saul again and again. At times, we feel disappointed and hurt by people, as well. In Psalm 13 David despaired, talked to God about what was going on in his life and his heart, and rose filled with faith and courage.

Psalm 13

"How long, Lord? Will You forget me forever? How long will You hide your face from me? How long must I wrestle with my thoughts and day after day have sorrow in my heart? How long will my enemy triumph over me? Look on me and answer, Lord my God. Give light to my eyes or I will sleep in death, and my enemy will say, "I have overcome him." And my foes will rejoice when I fall. But I trust in Your unfailing love, my heart rejoices in Your salvation. I will sing to the Lord praise, for He has been good to me."

David was saying "Lord, unless you give me some perspective here and peace in my heart, I don't think I can take it any longer." God gave him peace and perspective, and he remembered that God had indeed been good to him.

5. "I am the vine, and my Father is the gardener. He cuts off every branch in me that bears no fruit, while every branch that does bear fruit He prunes so that it will be even more fruitful" (John 15:1,2).

I	F	O	B	T	S	M
A	I	E	N	D	T	F.
T	T	B	F,	B	I	
V	G.	I	W	F	W	
A	H	M	E	H	B	
M	C	T	B	P	E	

6. "Weeping may remain for a night, but joy comes in the morning" (Psalm 30:5).

W	B
M	J
R	C
F	I
A	T
N,	M.

9

Reasons to Forgive

We Forgive Because God Says So

Have you ever answered your kids' quizzical need for explanations with "Just do it, because I said so?" Simply put, the first reason to forgive is God says so. He made us. He knows how we work. He has paid a high premium for forgiveness. He says so.

It sounds easy, doesn't it?

When we are in the nitty-gritty of real offense though, it isn't easy. A junior high coach picked one of my sons off the ground by the face mask of his football helmet and screamed into his face because he stepped over the side line. That hurt me so much I wanted to scale the fence and shake the guy's teeth out. It would have hurt and humiliated my son even more and I certainly would have dishonored the Lord, so I didn't. No, I didn't say anything then. But, I am embarrassed to tell you that scene occasionally played in my mind for years. It was partly because I didn't deal with it when I should have, and partly because I did not forgive this guy for a long time.

The offense formed a fence between me and God. That was dumb *and* dangerous. Whoever hurts us or our loved ones takes a piece of our past, but <u>only we can give them permission to take our today and our tomorrow.</u>

I should have spoken to that coach and to his superiors. I should have prayed for him, because he surely needed my prayer. Then I should have let it go. No doubt, the greatest times I have struggled to forgive have been when people have hurt my children. Yet, at times our children will be hurt, because we live in a world filled with offense.

We Forgive to be Forgiven

The second reason to forgive is to be forgiven by God. Forgiveness is the foundation upon which our faith rests. Both Matthew and Luke record Jesus' commanding words in the Lord's Prayer and provide us with this compelling reason to forgive. This is God's command and the way forgiveness works. God's words, not mine . . .

"For if you forgive men when they sin against you, your heavenly Father will also forgive you. But if you do not forgive men their sins, your Father will not forgive your sins" (Matthew 6:14, 15) and "Forgive us our sins, for we also forgive *everyone* who sins against us" (Luke 11:4 NIV).

"Forgive everyone, Lord?"

Yes, if you want freedom, everyone.

This implies that we are forgiving others when we ask God to forgive us.

Forgiving is present tense.

Forgiving is right now.

Forgiving is every day.

I ask for forgiveness. I extend forgiveness to others. When I am tempted to gripe and grouse about people and look down my nose at their sin, all I have to do is remember my own. I think of every selfish thought and every thoughtless word. This is a reality check for me.

It doesn't mean we don't recognize and at times confront sin that hurts people and the name of God. Though I don't like to, I have. Sometimes I have confronted sin the way God instructs me to - with love. At times, I have not. I need to be careful and always remember that I have been forgiven much.

As we pursue a life of forgiveness, because families in our culture inside and outside the church are filled with it, we need to address abuse. Abuse crosses all lines, male and female, rich and

86

poor, and all races and religions. Forgiveness is the divine vehicle to freedom in a sinful world, yet it does not justify sin. <u>If you find yourself in an abusive situation, the most loving act for you, the abuser, and your family is to face the truth.</u> Stop hiding the sin. Call it what it is and courageously seek help so you will not see this abuse perpetuated into the next generation. Perhaps you need to call authorities and/or get yourself and your children to a safe place. Seek help from a church. Get people praying for you! Abuse must be stopped for healing to begin. If you are in an abusive situation, get out of God's way. Pray for God to give you the wisdom to know what to do and the courage to do it! Then as an act of your will on your journey toward freedom, forgive.

We Forgive to Be Protected from the Evil One

The rest of Luke 11:4 reads, ". . . and lead us not into temptation, but deliver us from the evil one." Living a forgiveness-filled life protects us and our children from temptation from the evil one and from his blatant attack on our minds. Living a life of forgiveness protects our hearts and diminishes the enemy's power to turn us away from God.

I can't fly to the sun or I'll burn to nothingness, and I can't mock a holy God who says what He means and means what He says by rationalizing and justifying unforgiveness toward others. When I stray from abiding under God's protective care with a heart of unforgiveness, I give the enemy access to my heart.

That is why Paul urged the Corinthian church to forgive one another. He told them to forgive "in order that Satan might not outwit us, for we are not unaware of his schemes." We don't want to knowingly give the devil any wiggle room in our lives, so we forgive. God-fear is good fear, and the fear of the Lord was the beginning of wisdom for me. That God-fear mixed with His unimaginable sacrificial love beckons me to forgive.

Finding Freedom

1. The enemy tries to take advantage of us in many areas of our lives. Regarding offenses, worry, or fear, what lies does he use to lure you out from under God's covering of love?

2. There is only one weapon to fight the devil when he's dragging you out from under God's wings of protection, the word of God. It is our Sword. It is our only offensive weapon for this spiritual war. Read these scriptures regarding fear, worry, thoughts, and words. Read them out loud replacing the lies of the enemy with the truth of God's beautiful word.

   - *"For God has not given me a spirit of fear but of love, of power, and of a sound mind"* (2 Timothy 1:7). Paul was imprisoned for the last time when he wrote these words to Timothy. Nero was persecuting Christians with fervor by then, and Paul knew he would very soon be killed. So, he encouraged Timothy not to be afraid of those who would oppose him as he shared the gospel. The same fear that grips our gut and keeps us from sharing our faith with people and standing for truth is the same gut grabbing fear the devil snares us with in other areas. The threats against Paul and Timothy were very real. Paul reminded him that the opposite of fear was love and a sound mind. He reminded his young brother in Christ to run back under the protection of God's love. Unforgiveness produces fear rather than a sound mind in me. So, I forgive.

- *"I have been crucified with Christ and I no longer live but Christ lives in me. The life I live, I live by faith in the Son of God who loved me and gave His life for me"* (Galatians 2:20). This is who I am! I am not who I used to be. Christ lives in me! So, I forgive.

- *"May the words of my mouth and the meditations of my heart be pleasing to you, O Lord, my Rock and my Redeemer"* (Psalms 19:14). Offenses, worry, stress, disappointment, selfishness, and heartbreak draw me away from God's protection. As I learn to line up my thoughts and words with God's thoughts and words, I begin to rest in His love, and experience that sound mind of which Paul wrote. Yes, I forgive.

3. How might we respond to stressful 'life' issues?

→ Passive anger, rage, depression, binge eating, substance abuse, spending $$$
→ Which brings temporary relief from the stress
→ Followed by guilt, regret, and sometimes remorse
→ Then stress hits and the pattern begins again

We are hopeless to escape from these life patterns apart from our certainty that God loves us. Joining the spiritual fight and believing God's words changes our hearts and begins to break this cycle. When stress comes, instead of eating 3000 calories or raging at the kids, your spouse, or your mother, stop and speak the truth. *I need you, Lord. I can't do this without you. Help me to believe that*

90

I am who You made me to be. That honest cry ushers in the power of God.

Hide these words in your heart.

4. "For if you forgive men when they sin against you, your heavenly Father will also forgive you. But if you do not forgive men their sins, your Father will not forgive your sins" (Matthew 6:14, 15).

F	T	F	I	T	F
I	S	W	Y	S,	Y
Y	A	A	D	Y	S.
F	Y,	F	N	F	Matthew 6:14,15
M	Y	Y.	F	W	
W	H	B	M	N	

5. "Forgive us our sins, for we also forgive *everyone* who sins against us and lead us not into temptation, but deliver us from the evil one" (Luke 11:4).

F	F	E	U	N	D	E
U	W	W	A	I	U	O.
O	A	S	L	T,	F	Luke 11:4
S,	F	A	U	B	T	

10

If I Don't Forgive . . .

There is one more reason to forgive. In fact, it is the most important reason. First let's take a detour and look at what happens if we choose not to forgive.

There are many stories and scriptures that warn against unforgiveness. These verses sum it up. "Anyone who claims to be in the light but hates his brother is still in the darkness. Whoever loves his brother lives in the light, and there is nothing in him to make him stumble. But whoever hates his brother is in the darkness and walks around in the darkness. He does not know where he is going because the darkness has blinded him" (1 John 2:10,11).

Unforgiveness blinds us.

It keeps us in the dark.

Animosity toward others stops up our spiritual pipes. It hinders our fellowship with God and people. There have been times when my spiritual pipes became plugged because I took someone's offense. I wonder why I feel far from God, only to realize that I am holding animosity in my heart. An attitude of unforgiveness signals to God that I don't trust Him with my life or the lives of my loved ones. I forget that God hates injustice more than I do (Isaiah 34:8, 61:8). My unforgiveness is shouting to Him that He has somehow messed this thing up.

Unforgiveness won't help anyone and it won't bring about justice. It only tortures our souls by invading our thoughts, keeping the tentacles of the offender wrapped around us. Bitterness is based on feelings, and our feelings are exceedingly deceitful. They will fool us again and again. When I allow my feelings to lead, and follow my selfish flesh, God is *never* glorified.

God gives us many warnings in His word about unforgiveness. He made us in such a way that we cannot carry it or it grows into bitterness. Bitterness opens a door for the devil and hinders our ability to hear the voice of God. It can affect and destroy the relationships in our lives as well as our health. It hardens our hearts and makes us sick, both body and soul.

Simon's Bitterness

God gives us examples of folks who were impacted by bitterness. Simon was a Samaritan and a sorcerer who cast spells, worked magic, and everything that entails. The Bible tells us Simon believed the message of Christ. But, it also says that he was astonished by the miracles he saw the disciples performing and offered to pay them off to obtain this power. How in the world could he have missed the message of the cross so thoroughly? But he did, and so can we.

Peter replied, "May your money perish with you because you thought you could buy the gift of God with money. You have no part or share in this ministry, because your heart is not right before God. Repent of this wickedness and pray to the Lord. Perhaps He will forgive you for having such a thought in your heart. For, I see that you are full of bitterness and captive to sin" (Acts 8:19-23).

He was captive to sin. He was a prisoner to unforgiveness and full of bitterness. It had twisted his thinking. Though he wanted redemption, he didn't want to change. Maybe Simon thought, *"This is just the way I am! This is the way I will always be".*

Perhaps he had bitterness inside for so long he wasn't even aware of it. It prevented him from receiving the full grace and blessing of God. Bitterness toward *anyone* chains us to them. It chains our kids to them, too, because they take our offenses and embrace and mimic our attitudes toward others.

A Mama's Bitterness

I stood in the checkout line and looked at the guy in the line next to me. I thought, *dishonest jerk. He must be up to something.* The poor guy, he was probably just picking up a bottle of milk for his wife and I had him figured for Attila the Hun. Until I moved though my pain to forgiveness, I projected the motives or actions of the person who had hurt me onto others. Creepy, but that is what we sometimes do. That's what grief will do —it alters perspective.

I could have gone the way of Simon. As I moved through the stages of grief, anger was my companion for a season. I was hurt, and I was mad. If I'd had money I would have taken a hit out on every person in the grocery store who looked suspicious to me. Staying angry takes a lot of emotional energy though, and I couldn't stay there. I knew God loved me; I feared Him, too. So, before I felt like it, I made a *choice* to forgive.

I taught with a woman whose husband had left her. Though this had occurred many years earlier, she had not yet chosen forgiveness. She was bitter. Bitter parents often tell their children and others too much - so the world will know how violated they are. This places a burden on kids they are not meant to carry. Of course, the adversary of God loves it because it causes generation after generation to be poisoned with bitterness.

Though I did not really know her, one day after school I stood in the hall and politely listened as she told me a lot more about her life than I wanted to know. I was sad that one of her daughters was

95

present during this conversation. I was thankful my sons were not. She spewed out vile words about what we had in store for us. Though I was trying to be cordial, in my heart I was saying, "Get behind me, Satan!" I thought Jesus' words to Peter, who was trying to stop him from going to the cross, were an appropriate response to her poison.

I knew we would undoubtedly walk through tough circumstances as the fruit of divorce, and we did. But I was not going to let bitterness be one of them. The words she spoke and the selfish heart behind them were from the pit of hell. Unless this woman repented and cried out to God for help, a root of bitterness would take up residence in the hearts of her beautiful daughters. They would grow to become angry, contentious women like their momma.

These girls, like many kids, had watched what led to the end of their parents' marriage. They were pieces of the land mine that had flown in a thousand directions when their family split. These beautiful girls had seen their mother seethe with bitterness. Sadly though, they had not seen her grab onto God's gracious love through the fire. They had not learned from their mother how to forgive.

Finding Freedom

1. Like Simon, do I tend to hold onto the same old ways of handling life?

2. Am I willing to let God show me what bitterness is doing to my life?

3. Am I willing to let Him show me some new things about forgiveness?

4. We might think, *"This is just the way I am! This is the way I will always be"*! If this is your thinking, how has it hindered God from helping you grow and from healing you?

5. Unforgiveness will make us sick. It will give us wrinkles! That high stressor keeps the hormone, cortisol, pouring into our bodies. It produces the opposite effect of laughter, love, or exercise which helps us fight disease and gives us a feeling of wellbeing. Do you feel the effects of unforgiveness in your physical body, or do you know someone whose health is being affected by years of unforgiveness? What does it look like?

6. There are two doors between you and anyone who has hurt you. You can unlock your side. The other door is between them and the Lord and is not your business. What are the doors of unforgiveness that you need to open to walk toward freedom?

Hide these words in your heart.

7. We forgive because, "Anyone who claims to be in the light but hates his brother is still in the darkness. Whoever loves his brother lives in the light, and there is nothing in him to make him stumble. But whoever hates his brother is in the darkness and walks around in the darkness. He does not know where he is going because the darkness has blinded him" (1 John 2:10,11).

A	H	B	I	B	D.	T
W	B	L	H	I	H	D
C	I	I	T	I	D	H
T	S	T	M	T	N	B
B	I	L,	H	D	K	H.
I	T	A	S.	A	W	
T	D.	T	B	W	H	
L	W	I	W	A	I	
B	L	N	H	I	G	
H	H		H	T	B	

99

11

Bitterness

Unforgiveness left unattended turns into bitterness. Satan manipulates us into bitterness any time we give him opportunity because he knows it distorts our view of life and keeps us from moving forward. If I took a gulp of vinegar and swallowed it, it would burn all the way down. Gulping vinegar burns our esophagus, and harboring bitterness burns our lives and the lives of those watching us. Bitterness, like other sin, won't disappear on its own. It remains with us until it's dealt with, a silent poison that becomes more toxic with each passing year.

How many of us know people who have become bitter? Maybe one of our parents is bitter or a sibling or friend. You can often spot a bitter person by the words coming out of their mouth, the expression on their face and certainly their attitude toward life. Bitterness renders everyone the enemy even if it is the grocer or the dog. Bitterness listens to lies and believes them. Bitterness manipulates, harbors bitter thoughts, *and* justifies it. Bitterness takes vengeance into its own hands, even if it is only in one's thoughts. No one is more tormented by bitterness though, than the soul harboring it. It holds them in a place of hurt, abandonment, and violation.

What is bitterness?

It is sin.

Regarding sin, Jesus said if your hand causes you to sin cut it off. If your eye causes you to sin put it out. He was not telling us to literally cut off a hand or put out an eye, but He was illustrating the seriously destructive nature of sin left to seed in the lives of His children.

Think about it. A surgeon seeking to eradicate cancer does not remove part of the cancer. He removes all the cancer and some of the tissue around it. A farmer doesn't pick the top off weeds in his field. He yanks them out by the roots or poisons them. He doesn't let weeds go, or they will blow all over his field and the problem spreads. When unforgiveness goes to seed, it grows deep roots and spreads.

Don't Take the Trash to Bed

We can't miss Paul's point in Ephesians 4:26, 27. "In your anger do not sin. Do not let the sun go down while you are still angry, and do not give the devil a foothold"—meaning, a hold on your heart. How many times have we gone to bed mad at someone? Think about it. One night of unforgiveness will give the devil a place to stand in our heart and mind. Because he will take every inch of ground we yield to him, imagine how much ground he takes in months or years of bitterness. Because bitterness destroys lives Ephesians 4:31 reads, "Get rid of all bitterness, rage and anger, brawling and slander along with every other form of malice." That verse reads *all* bitterness.

Not some of it.

Not part of it.

As I write this week, how like God to give me a great illustration of the stink of bitterness. We have a dead buzzard in our garbage can. No kidding. He died in our neighbor's yard. Don didn't have time to bury the little guy so he canned him. Needless to say, I am counting the hours until the truck comes down our street to pick up that garbage. It's the stinkiest thing I've ever smelled. So is bitterness.

Kind, Tender, Forgiving – That's Not Bitterness

Let's look at the opposite to bitterness. Ephesians 4:32 reads, "Be kind one to another, tenderhearted, forgiving one another, even as God for Christ's sake has forgiven you." We are forgiven much, yet bitterness so fills us that we have little capacity to be kind and compassionate. Bitterness won't make room for the sweetness of God in us. If I find it difficult to be compassionate and kind, perhaps I need to change direction.

We get rid of garbage every week so the house won't stink. And we forgive regularly like we throw out the garbage. If we hold onto offenses, it stinks up our lives and the lives of those we love. Bitterness hurts us, others, and the name of God, so we must call it what it is.

Sin.

Then repent.

To repent is making the *choice* to change direction. When we choose to turn, the chains begin to fall off. Elisabeth Elliot counseled us to mortify sin. Kill it. Don't manage it. Nothing has the power to release the heaviness inside us like facing the truth, repenting, and changing direction. Through God's amazing love and grace, we can look at that weed, call it a weed, and pull it up. That's when the devil loses advantage or control of that part of our heart, so that kindness, compassion, and *more* forgiveness can flow through us to our world.

Finding Freedom

1. Bitterness will sabotage lives. For an eye opener, look up the synonyms for the word sabotage.

2. Do you know someone whose unforgiveness has gone to seed? What does that look like in their lives? In their relationships?

3. Can I think of someone right now that makes my mind swirl or stomach sick as I ponder how unfair they were?

4. Could that unresolved hurt, that deep wound have grown a root of bitterness?

5. Have I done what I need to do to make past offences against others right? If not, what do I need to do?

6. Could bitterness be affecting those I love and other relationships in my life? Search your heart. How has it affected your life and the lives of those you love?

7. Look up Hebrews 12:14, 15 and write it in your own words.

   Hide these words in your heart.

8. "In your anger do not sin. Do not let the sun go down while you are still angry. And do not give the devil a foothold" (Ephesians 4:26,27).

I	D	D	A	A
Y	N	W	D	F.
A	L	Y	N	
D	T	A	G	
N	S	S	T	
S.	G	A.	D	

106

"Get rid of all bitterness, rage and anger, brawling and slander, along with every form of malice. Be kind and compassionate to one another, forgiving each other, just as in Christ God forgave you" (Ephesians 4:31,32).

G	A,	F	T	A
R	B	O	O	I
O	A	M.	A,	C
A	S,	B	F	G
B,	A	K	E	F
R	W	A	O,	Y.
A	E	C	J	

Ephesians 4:31,32

12

Three Forgivenesses

Elisabeth Elliot said, "A lifetime of obediences is a lifetime of 'forgivenesses.'" Bad grammar . . . good theology. Bitter or better, that is our choice. To choose better we must choose three forgivenesses: to forgive others, to receive forgiveness for ourselves, and to forgive God.

Forgiving Others

There are many stories of people who have chosen to forgive and have learned that freedom is found in forgiveness. A man or woman forgiving a spouse's unfaithfulness, children forgiving a parent for leaving, a daughter forgiving a mother or father for abuse, a sexually abused child choosing to forgive his or her attacker. I know these stories of forgiveness, because I know the people to whom they belong. Their forgiveness, like Christ's, shows us the way and gives *us* courage to forgive.

A mother who was finding her way to freedom shared her story with me. She struggled with rage and anger. It had dominated her life, and her choices had led to decades of substance abuse and broken relationships.

I asked, "Who are you mad at?"

She relayed her story of being sexually abused. It had destroyed a piece of her heart. We talked about the perpetrator. I was surprised but she seemed to have genuinely forgiven him.

"So, who are you mad at?" I asked again.

"At my mother," she said, "My mother should have protected me."

Yes, her mother should have protected her. This young mom like so many who have been abused as children carried fear, sadness, and rage in her soul because the person or people who should have protected her failed to. She had therefore spent a lifetime looking for love in all the wrong places.

When anything or anyone got near her broken heart, she exploded. People and circumstances would often innocently trigger feelings of betrayal from her childhood, ripping the wounds open again and again. She had no idea why she was mad all the time. She had no idea that her unforgiveness had chained her to the person who had hurt her. As we talked, she learned that she didn't have to *feel* forgiveness to forgive. I told her that I had learned that feelings follow faith, not the other way around.

Forgiving her mother for knowing about her abuse and doing nothing about it, did not justify what her mother did. Forgiving her mother, like forgiving the perpetrator, would set this young mother's heart free. It begins with that first act of our will to let go of the offender - to talk right out loud to God about it and to *choose* forgiveness.

Once we forgive, that hurt might well up in us again. When that ache in our chest and tormenting thoughts try to invade, we again give the object of our hurt to God. Speak what God says, that we are forgiven, that we have forgiven, and that we are no longer chained to our offender and their sin.

She and I began to pray. I spoke. Then she followed. She admitted a lifetime of anger, resentment, and unforgiveness toward her mother and others which had led to rage, destructive relationships, addiction, and brokenness. She asked God to forgive her sin and to help her forgive others.

Then she finally said, "I forgive her."

110

Through that day and into many days that followed, feelings of resentment returned and tormented her mind. Yet she said over and over, "I forgive her." Time passed and one evening as she was driving home from work still saying, "I forgive," suddenly she began saying, "Lord, forgive her. Lord, please forgive her."

Forgiveness begins a change in us.

Forgiveness ultimately will set us free.

Receiving Forgiveness for Yourself

It was hidden, not a part of my past I wanted anyone to know, least of all my sons. I had been a Christian school teacher for decades, was raising kids, and taught the Bible to women. Only God and my husband were privy to that dark month of my life - the month I made the choice to take the life of my first child.

A few weeks before school was out that year, my friend Rhonda, and I were in the teacher's work room. In the middle of our conversation I blurted out, "When I was nineteen I had an abortion. I need to share it with these kids if only to save one baby's life."

I immediately thought, *"What in the world made those words come out of my mouth"?* I had no intention of talking about this!

God's intentions became clear though. It was the rest of my story. I wasn't going to run from it any longer. I had to share it if only to save one baby. My dear sons, Chris, Parker, and Trent would have to know. Fear and sadness rose in my chest. I thought, *"Lord, it will break their hearts."* I told Don what God wanted me to do.

I cried.

111

He prayed.

I cried more.

Pandora's Box flew open. A flood of memories escaped from hidden places of a college kid from Texas sitting alone on a late night flight from Houston to New York City.

Fear.

Loneliness.

Shame.

Sorrow.

I had to remember.

I cried more.

He prayed more.

That summer, I sat through shame and tears. One at a time, I told my sons what I had done. That summer, they cried too, and they forgave. At some point during that summer, I began to receive forgiveness for myself, as well.

Less than six months after my "blurting out" incident in the workroom, I stood before hundreds of high school kids, many of whom had been my students, and I told my story. I was nervous but determined, and as I walked into the gym Trent and his friends whispered, "We are praying for you." There is no doubt in my mind that at least one baby was saved that day.

Maybe you have asked God to forgive you and have asked those you have hurt for forgiveness, yet your past continues to flood your mind with condemnation. Like me, maybe there are things you have done that you regret horribly, or voices from your childhood lying to you. Like me, maybe there are some things you need to do, or some people you need to talk with on your journey toward freedom.

Listen for God's voice. Do what He tells you. Talk with the people He brings to mind. Then check the source of that condemnation. Whose voice would remind you of sin that Christ, the Messiah, the Creator, the Redeemer, the Lord, the God of the Universe paid for with His very blood? This is not the voice of your loving God. These are the voices of demons. The Bible tells us Satan is the accuser of the brothers and sisters. Yes, Satan is the accuser. If he isn't able to trip us up with habitual sin, he'll cripple us with false guilt.

Identify the accuser, call him a liar, and remind yourself whose you are. You are a child of the living God, not because of your merit but because of what Jesus Christ did for you on the cross.

Therefore, receive God's forgiveness for yourself.

"How great is the love the Father has lavished on us; that we should be called children of God" (I John 3:1). We are his children, and are ". . . sealed with the Holy Spirit of promise, which is an earnest of our inheritance, unto the redemption of God's own possession, unto the praise of his glory" (Ephesians 1:13b, 14).

If Christ died for the world, Christ died for us! We are His children! So, we *repent* and weep with sorrow over our offenses to God and man. We *release* our guilt and sorrow to Jesus, and we *receive* His forgiveness.

We repent.

We release.

We receive.

Then when we hear the voices of condemnation whisper *or* scream through our thoughts, we remember whose we are and remind the accuser of the blood of Jesus that has washed us as white as snow.

Forgiving God

This sounds like blasphemy, doesn't it? Let me explain. We choose to forgive others. We choose to receive forgiveness for ourselves. But what about God? Though God doesn't need forgiving for anything, He gets blamed for a lot of things. Because blaming God for the sorrows of our lives may have commandeered our hearts, perhaps we need to also forgive God.

Jeremiah' Heart

Jerusalem was decimated. The Jews had been taken into captivity because they were utterly wicked. Jeremiah mourned. His heart was broken over the sin of his people. He had warned them, counseled them, and prayed for them. For obeying God, he endured abuse and ridicule. Now he sadly watched as Jerusalem become a detestable place and was finally destroyed.

The Bible says Jeremiah cried so much over the sin of his people and God's judgment on them that he couldn't even see. Have you ever cried until your eyes were swollen shut? That was Jeremiah. What happen to Jerusalem, its people, and to him was horrible, and he laid some blame on God.

In the book of Lamentations, the prophet looked back. "Is it nothing to you, all you who pass by? Look around and see. Is any suffering like my suffering that was afflicted on me that the Lord brought on me in the day of His fierce anger?" (Lamentations 1:12).

Though he had been faithful, no one had listened to Jeremiah. Everything was lost, and he felt utterly alone.

Like Jeremiah, when we're hurting we feel alone.

My Heart

Early one spring I had to deal with this in my heart. The boys were out with friends, and I was in the house cooking dinner. It probably included Hamburger Helper. We ate a lot of Hamburger Helper. The deep throb in my heart was gone but it still ached. I had stopped running. I had concluded that I was not going to make big bucks for the boys and me. I would take one day at a time and try to be the best momma and teacher I could.

Tears ran down my cheeks as I washed a few dishes and stirred up some dinner. Suddenly the floodgate opened. I crumpled down on the floor.

I wailed.

Not a cry I recognized.

So deep.

Mournful.

"Lord, it's You I'm mad at. We tried to be faithful. We put our trust in You. Why did You let this happen? Why did You let this happen?"

There, I said it.

Six months earlier the bottom fell out of what I called marriage. I was shell-shocked. My husband had not lived with us for twelve years. Yes, twelve years, but he and I were still legally married. Right up until it all crumbled around us, I believed that someday he *would* come home. I couldn't give up the ship. It was a lack of faith to do so. When it was suddenly over, I blamed God. Not out loud though. Just in my heart.

God knows everything and I don't. I knew that. He loves me with a love I can't understand. I knew that. I wanted to trust Him, but this hurt so much. It seemed impossible to recognize His loving hand through the fog of pain.

Since my husband had been absent for a long time our circumstances changed very little after the divorce.

Something died though.

Hope died.

My hope that he would ever come home was gone. I was embarrassed. I was afraid to say it. But in the secrets of my heart, I blamed God. Lying on the floor in my kitchen wailing while dinner bubbled on the stove, I peeled my hands off one more thing.

God to Dana:

"Dana, I have been waiting for you to talk to me about this. You blame me. Your pain and unanswered questions made you push Me away. That mournful cry pouring out from your heart is grief over the ocean you put between us. We are finally talking about what's going on in your heart. That's good. No more ocean. I'm still in you, Dana, still with you, a whisper away. Now let's get down to healing your heart and the hearts of your children."

Truth.

We had to start with the truth. I didn't know that what I called faith and long-suffering had become co-dependency. We can prop up the sin of those we love by making excuses, cleaning up the mess behind them, and pretending it's okay. That's what I did.

My unwillingness to let go of my husband was a lack of faith. I wouldn't give him to God. God therefore gave me the push I needed the summer before.

I loved to teach, but I loved being at home with my family more than anything. It reminded me of the sweet summers I had as a child. Like my teacher mom, it was great joy to give my family the best of my time and energy in the summer.

That peaceful summer ran aground though, when I began receiving disturbing phone calls late at night. Through conversations with one of my husband's friends, details of the past twelve or thirteen years were revealed to me. I didn't want to be in this soap opera. But I was, and that was the truth.

It broke my heart.

I felt stupid.

But I had to go there.

Whatever your truth is, God will walk with you through it as He did with me. I also had to get out of the way. I do not fully understand all it took for the Lord to penetrate my first husband's heart, but the first step was for me to get out of God's way.

I also had to forgive.

Obedience had nothing to do with my feelings. As an act of my will, forgiveness was the only way to move forward. The feelings followed.

When my marriage ended, I had to choose three forgivenesses:

- I had to forgive Gregg for breaking our hearts.
- I had to receive forgiveness for myself for my stupidity and any part my sin played in the demise of my marriage.
- I had to forgive God for letting it all happen.

Remember those chapters in the Bible where Jeremiah wept and blamed God for the calamity that came upon Israel? "I remember my affliction and my wandering, the bitterness and the gall. I will remember them, and my soul is downcast within me" (Lamentations 3:20).

In the next verse his mood changes. "Yet this I call to mind and therefore I have hope."

There is that word again.

Hope.

One word.

A changed perspective.

He had wept and cried for all that was lost. Then He remembered God. "Because of the Lord's great love, we are not consumed, for his compassions never fail. They are new every morning; great is your faithfulness" (Lamentations 3:22, 23). This faithful and compassionate man suffered because he saw the sin of his people, knew it would cause their destruction, and watched them be destroyed. Yet, when He *remembered* God it helped him make sense of it all.

When I remembered God, it helped me to make sense of it all too. My honest and tearful time of truth with the Lord that evening on my kitchen floor helped me remember His loving character. He is my Father and He nailed his only Son, Jesus, to a cross for me.

Finding Freedom

1. Do you need to forgive yourself for choices you have made in the past? What is it that holds you in bondage that you need to forgive and let go?

2. Have you ever been mad at God for allowing something to happen to you or yours? What was it?

3. We may try to keep things from spiraling out of control by holding frantically onto the status quo. However, is there someone or some situation that you need to move away from? What situation or person might you need to get away from so God can do His work in their life?

Hide these words in your heart.

4. You are a child of God.

"How great is the love the Father has lavished on us; that we should be called children of God" (1 John 3:1).

```
H  T    U    C
G  F    T    C
I  H    W    O
T  L    S    G.
L  O    B
```

5.You are God's very possession!" You were also included in Christ when you heard the message of truth, the gospel of your salvation sealed with the Holy Spirit of promise, which is an earnest of our inheritance, unto the redemption of God's own possession, unto the praise of His glory" (Ephesians 1:13b,14).

```
Y    T    S    A    G
W    M    W    E    O
A    O    T    O    P,
I    T    H    O    U
I    T    S    I,   T
C    G    O    U    P
W    O    P,   T    O
Y    Y    W    R    H
H    S    I    O    G.
```

6.Because of the Lord's great love for you, you have hope!

"I remember my affliction and my wandering, the bitterness and the gall. I will remember them, and my soul is downcast within me. Yet this I call to mind and therefore I have hope; Because of the Lord's great love we are not consumed, for His compassions never fail. They are new every morning; great is thy faithfulness." (Lamentations 3:19-23).

I	T	R	W	M	B	W	C	E
R	B	T,	M.	A	O	A	N	M;
M	A	A	Y	T	T	N	F.	G
A	T	M	T	I	L	C,	T	I
A	G.	S	I	H	G	F	A	T
M	I	I	C	H;	L	H	N	F.
W, W	D	T						

Lamentations 3:19-23

13

Forgive for Love

Injustice.

Pain.

Bitterness.

Retribution.

Forgiveness.

Freedom.

Through the ages these recurring themes are found in literature because they are exemplified in all humanity. JeanValjean in "Les Miserables" was cruelly abused for most of his life. His crime - he was hungry. His bitterness and hatred ran deep.

What about Ebenezer Scrooge in Dickens "Christmas Carol"? The hole his lonely childhood left in his heart made him selfish and bitter indeed. How can we forget the image of Scrooge's partner, Marley, who came back from the dead to warn Ebenezer donning chains he had forged in a life devoted to self? Each Christmas when I watch the "Christmas Carol" I think of the chains forged around the lives of those who walk in unforgiveness. Each time I see "Les Miserables" I think of the power of love to set captives free.

These fictional characters found their way to freedom. For Jean and Ebenezer, perspective, forgiveness, and freedom all arrived in the same package. The highest of all reasons to forgive. The same reason Jesus forgave us – for love.

The unconditional love of a priest for Valjean. The relentless devotion of a nephew and loving service of Bob Cratchit for Scrooge. When these broken and embittered men opened their eyes to the love around them, they forgave and the heaviness they carried in their souls fell away.

In forgiving, we open the door of our hearts to Christ's love and the love around us. In forgiving we free ourselves to pour that love out to our world. Only in forgiving can we follow Jesus, and only in following Jesus can we spread the light of His love to our world.

Think of Christ's exhortation when he said, "Take up your cross daily and follow me" (Luke 9:23). He spoke this command to his disciples right after he told them He would be rejected and killed. He was saying, "I'm leaving, boys. I'm leaving carrying my cross. If you want to follow me, you'll have to carry your cross too."

I have thought a lot about what the cross signifies. In the first century AD the Romans reserved crucifixion for non-Romans. It was such a cruel method of execution that Roman citizens were not subjected to it. Though shocking, in this century we are again seeing crucifixion of Christians and others in certain regions of the world.

The description we read in the Bible of Christ's crucifixion was typical of Roman execution. The prisoner was beaten. The burdensome beam was placed on his ripped and torn neck and shoulders and bound to his arms. He was then forced to carry the beam to the execution site. This cruelty was intended to bring those in the Roman Empire into subjection.

It did.

It was intended to cause humiliation, pain, and suffering.

It did.

Yet, Jesus tells us to take up *our* cross and follow Him.

He endured cruelty, humiliation, and great suffering knowing that living on this planet was going to be hard for me. He took up his cross first, so I would. He said, "Come to me, all you who are weary and burdened, and I will give you rest. Take my yoke upon you and learn from me, for I am gentle and humble in heart, and you will find rest for your souls. For my yoke is easy and my burden is light" (Matthew 11:28-30). The greatest burden I must lie down to rest in Him is unforgiveness of offenses against me and mine.

He can handle my burdens.

That is why He came.

When I give Jesus the heaviness I have carried in my soul, I am taking up my cross and following Him. Living means we've been hurt by others. So, in this offensive and sinful world the only way to leave bitterness behind is to forgive - daily.

Every day.

Sometimes - many times each day.

"'Then Peter came to Jesus and asked, "Lord, how many times shall I forgive my brother or sister who sins against me? Up to seven times?' Jesus answered, 'I tell you, not seven times, but seventy-seven times'" (Matthew 18:21, 22).

My response to daily offense, perhaps above all other things, shows where I am in my relationship to God. I heard this expressed in a teaching and it hit me between the eyes. "Any offense I have taken toward those who have offended me is perhaps more serious to God than what has been done to me." That stung my heart a bit, but I believe it is true.

Why?

Because God knows what bitterness does to the human heart, so he showed us how it works. His response to offense right up to the moment he died on the cross was grace, not retribution. He looked down at the soldiers who were gambling for his clothes, probably the same ones who had driven the nails into his hands. And he cried out, "Forgive them, for they know not what they do" (Luke 23:34). He forgave those who had tortured him, had blasphemed the name of God, and were now killing him.

He granted them (and us) undeserved mercy. That frees us to in turn grant undeserved mercy to those who have hurt us, "bear(ing) with each other and forgive(ing) whatever grievances you may have against one another. Forgive as the Lord forgave you" (Colossians 3:13).

We can't do this without God's gracious help. It must be done by His Spirit, because this kind of forgiveness is not natural. It's supernatural. From the cross Jesus was asking us, "Do you want to be free? Do you want to live in peace and with purpose? Then forgive."

We can have no part in the cross until we *choose* to forgive.

Mercy – Grace – Forgiveness – Freedom – The Peace of Christ

Finding Freedom

1. Read John14:27 and Luke 1:78, 79. What has Christ left you? Forgive and walk in this freedom!

Because of the cross, we are free to forgive. God's power to forgive rests on you. Hide these words in your heart.

2. "But he said to me, "My grace is sufficient for you, for my power is made perfect in weakness." Therefore I will boast all the more gladly about my weaknesses, so that Christ's power may rest on me." (2 Corinthians 12:9).

B	G	M	W.	T	S	O
H	I	P	T	M	T	M,
S	S	I	I	G	C	2 Corinthians 12:9
T	F	M	W	A	P	
M, Y,	P	B	M	M		
M	F	I	A	W,	R	

127

3.Forgive so you can love.

"Therefore, as God's chosen people, holy and dearly loved, clothe yourselves with compassion, kindness, humility, gentleness, and patience. Bear with each other and forgive one another. If any of you have grievance against someone, forgive as the Lord forgave you. And over all these virtues put on love, which binds them all together in perfect unity (Colossians 3:12-14).

T	A	C	B	O	H	T	A	W
A	D	K	W	A.	G	L	T	B
G	L,	H	E	I	A	F	V	T
C	C	G	O	A	S,	Y.	P	A
P,	Y	A	A	O	F	A	O	T
H	W	P.	F	Y	A	O	L	I
								P
								U

4. Forgive and receive rest for your soul.

"Come to me all you who are weary and burdened and I will give you rest. Take my yoke upon you and learn from me, for I am gentle and humble in heart and you will find rest for your souls. For my yoke is easy and my burden is light" (Matthew 11:28-30).

C	A	W	Y	M,	H	F	M	B
T	W	G	U	F	I	R	Y	I
M	A	Y	Y	I	H	F	I	L.
A	B	R.	A	A	A	Y	E	
Y	A	T	L	G	Y	S.	A	
W	I	M	F	A	W	F	M	

Conclusion

We may have a heart filled with hidden hurt. Years after great loss we may be stuck in sorrow or anger. We may isolate ourselves, be perpetually discontent, burn bridges, or always seem to have an enemy. If that is where we live, then we probably have sat down in the middle of perceived or true grief. The bleeding in our soul from a deep wound is crying to get out.

Through the sorrows of life, we will either become bitter or better. We choose either the way of the cross toward God, or the endlessly empty way of self. Years after being saved by the blood of Jesus, many of us are still living in the shadow of Marah—the shadow of bitterness. As we look at our lives in Christ, might we ask, "Have I left bitterness behind?" If we haven't, then like Simon and that bitter momma, our sin holds us at arm's length from God. Yet, God wants to pull us in close.

We deal with our past but we don't camp there. Christ's love is deeper than that. He died for much more. If this is where we find ourselves, today we can choose to forgive. We were saved to let the light and love of Jesus Christ shine for our world. We have the power of the Holy Spirit in us to enable us to forgive and in forgiving we will find peace.

Through gritted teeth and tears, for the sake of Jesus who died on the cross *and* for those you love, relinquish all to the Lord.

Forgive.

God can heal us and help us, but we must let Him.

If the adversary of God has held this part of our hearts for perhaps a lifetime, we will be in for a fight. But it's worth the fight. In Psalm 77 the writer cries out to God. In *The Message,* it reads, "I yell out to my God, I yell with all my might. I yell at the top of my lungs. He listens. I found myself in trouble and went looking for my Lord; my life was an open wound that wouldn't heal . . ."

Like the Psalmist we can talk to God about the deep hurts of our heart. We can go to our closet, behind the garage, out to a field, or sit in our car in a parking lot. We reach back, think through, pray through, and cry through every offense against us or ours, right up to today. We can ask God to forgive us for holding onto offences and allowing them to twist our thoughts and responses to life and to those we love. Then we cry out to God for the grace and courage to forgive any who have hurt us and to take our bitterness away.

You will probably need someone to walk alongside you as you travel the path to forgiveness. If you need help, get help! Find a friend, teacher, pastor, neighbor, or counselor to hold you, help you, and pray you through—no matter how long it takes. Once you lay the bitterness down and forgive, the anger will begin to melt away.

God can either remove sad memories or heal them in such a way that when we fully forgive we can remember the offense without feeling great pain.

Forgiving   releases us to freely receive God's love and takes us to a place of freedom present only in those who are forgiven and who choose to forgive.

If Jesus is God, and if the virgin birth, Christ's perfect life, the cross of Christ, the resurrection and ascension, and the assurance that God is coming back are true—and they are true—then God can help you, heal you, and through His gracious love set you free.

We will face injustice in this fallen world. But we are ambassadors for Christ Jesus, and we are here to draw others to Him by our love. His message of forgiveness is the most powerful display of His love. There is no greater gift we can give ourselves or our world than to trust God enough to walk in the freedom of forgiveness.

Made in the USA
Columbia, SC
19 June 2019